The Swirling Tide

by
Josephine Newman

third house

First published in the United Kingdom 2010
By Third House Publishing

The Swirling Tide

Printed in England by Lightning Source.

ISBN 978-1-907695-00-1

Third House Publishing,
21 Laceys Lane
Exning
Newmarket
Suffolk
CB8 7HL

Disclaimer

All the events, places and the people detailed in this book are all real.
However, in order to protect the innocent and others, I have changed most
of the names and I have kept the exact location undisclosed.

Dedication

This book is dedicated to the memory of my parents.

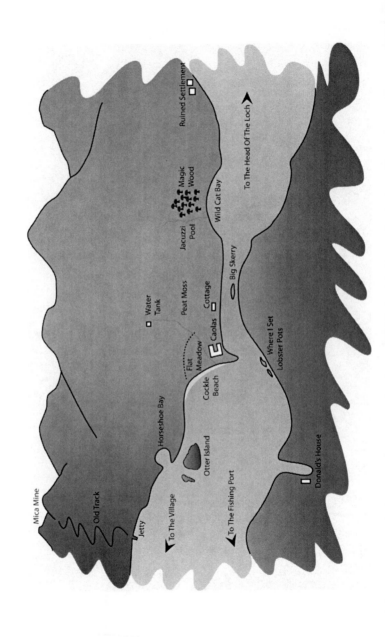

Chapter One

No Road, No Electricity and No Telephone

The water, boiling hot and icy cold, gushed and gurgled out of the two huge, old, tarnished Victorian taps into the deep, long, cast iron bath. It was the colour of matured whisky and smelt of hot peat, for this water came straight off the mountain behind the house. None of your filtered and chemically bug free treated water here; this was possibly full of microscopic beasties and certainly the occasional piece of dead grass, but was sweet, soft and incredibly refreshing to drink.

Various candles, lopsided in their containers, cast a flickering glow with deep shadows to the steamy bathroom. These candles had nothing to do with creating a romantic ambiance to the occasion; they were necessary for light as there was no electricity in this house. In fact, there was no electricity for miles and miles in any direction and only a small amount of light from the evening sun filtered through the small deep set window.

A generous quantity of bubble bath poured into the surging water foamed into candy floss peaks and I anticipated submerging myself up to my chin in hot water and warming up, for it was cold outside and a house without electricity does not have central heating. The luxury of piping hot water came from the Rayburn burning in the kitchen.

I was about to step into the inviting water, when suddenly something long, thin, black and solid erupted out of the cold tap and splashed noisily into the water. In shock, I withdrew

1

my hovering foot, for whatever had just arrived in my bathtub was very much alive. Hastily scooping copious armfuls of foam out of the bath and onto the wooden floor, I could make out a long sinuous shiny snake, right where I was about to sit. A SNAKE in my tub! I yelped and jumped back, before common sense prevailed and I realised that there are no jet black snakes in Western Scotland. Thrashing around in the warm water was a foot long eel. It writhed amongst the bubbles, dark and vibrant. I quickly turned off the taps.

Have you ever tried to catch a healthy eel with your bare hands? Nor had I until that moment. When I tried grabbing it, its slimy body wound sinuously around my arm. A washing up bowl failed miserably to contain the creature. It just flowed effortlessly over the rim and back to flounder around the bath. I was not going to waste all that sumptuous hot water by draining it away. A large colander hastily grabbed from the kitchen did the trick. The water quickly drained away and this beautiful creature was for the moment captured. I threw a small towel over the top to keep it in and rushed naked from the house across the farm yard to the burn, which runs past the buildings, where it I tipped the angry, thrashing eel out into the gurgling water and it regained its freedom.

Standing for a minute by the rocky bank, I mused that this creature, born in the warm Sargasso sea so far away, but not as hot as my bath, had travelled the Atlantic Ocean, swum right up the long sea loch, then nearly a mile up the steep burn and into the water tank high on the hill, to eventually slither down the old iron water pipe into the house and flop into my bath.

The wind keened through the old ash tree by the burn and I shivered. There was no danger of anyone seeing me nude there in the fading rays of the sun, for the nearest neighbour lived three miles away on the other side of the loch. It was time to go in and shut the door, enjoy a soapy wallow and chuckle that for a fleeting moment I had really believed that there was a Black Mamba in my bath.

This amusing memory often comes back to me, for this happened many years ago when my husband Pete and I lived in a remote farmhouse, accessible only by boat many miles up a lonely loch in Western Scotland.

I will take you back to the beginning, for we had many adventures there.

You could ask what would possess two reasonably sane early middle-aged people to abandon fairly well paid, secure jobs and a comfortable, centrally heated house and choose to move six hundred miles or so further north, to live in a remote, draughty old house with no electricity, phone or even road. Was it an impetuous mid life crisis, or a feeling for a new adventure?

For me it all started with a love for the area carried with me since I was ten. My parents had taken me on holiday to Western Scotland and on a beautiful, sun kissed day, we were taking a boat trip out along the coast. I can remember that I always questioned where I was, which loch it was and what mountain that was.

My father showed me how to read maps; a fascination that I still have to this day.

"That is all wilderness in there."

He had gestured with his arm and swept his hand around to indicate the sea loch penetrating deep into the distant jumble of rugged blue purple peaks.

"You will never be able to get into there as there are no roads and it's very remote," he added.

I still remember the effect those words had on me. It was like a magnet to me, this inaccessible area that could only be reached by boat or a couple of hard days' hiking in from the nearest road. The lure of this place, this wilderness where deer far outnumbered humans never waned, but for many years it just seemed like a distant dream. One day I vowed that I would walk in there, camp and explore.

When it did happen more than twenty years later, I was not disappointed. In fact my passion for the area became stronger. I read all I could, its turbulent history and I became acquainted with some of the people living there in the isolated communities. Over several more years I went back and discovered high and lonely places; beautiful hidden gems of lochans and glens full of wild red deer.

My husband Pete joined me in loving the area and a suggestion gradually evolved to seek work there. Several years later, amazingly, the opportunity arose. New owners had bought a whole vast tract of wilderness hills and glens and there were changes afoot and opportunities for new employment.

The job description was to live in an un-modernised house over ten miles down a pathless loch. The successful applicant would have to rebuild a ruined cottage, to modernise and completely alter the old house and to assist in running a stalking estate of some ten thousand acres. To be competent in handling a boat was essential, as that was the only way in and out for people, building materials and food. People applying for the job had to be self sufficient and resourceful as there was no road, telephone or electricity.

Every bag of cement, piece of timber, nuts, bolts and tools would have to come fifty miles by narrow roads from the nearest building merchant, to the fishing port and then on by boat. The next door neighbours would be living three miles down the loch one way and five miles up at the head of the loch the other way. The nearest telephone was six miles away in the village.

"You must be mad," some of our friends exclaimed, whilst others said wistfully that they wished they had the courage to embark on such an adventure. The opportunity to leave all the crowded motorways, crime and the fast pace of life and work in such a pristine environment seemed like heaven to us.

"Why not?" we countered. The time seemed right, as our daughter was due to go off to university for three years and we had no other ties. It was time to do something completely different, take up a challenge. The opportunity might never arise again. We had the skills necessary, but were we tough enough? Did messing about in boats some years back qualify us to take a boat out on the open sea? One good friend with a lifetime of ocean sailing was horrified. We assured him we would quickly learn.

Our prospective employer, who had recently purchased this stalking estate, was satisfied with our references, encouraged by our joint enthusiasm for his plans and after an interview in Scotland we heard that we had got the job. We were ecstatic, but also just a little apprehensive at the huge challenge that we had accepted.

"When do you want us to start?" we asked.

"As soon as possible," was his reply.

The removal lorry stood swaying in the fierce gusts of wind on the pier at the end of the road. It was 10.30am and the previous two days had been virtually sleepless for us. There had been a busy day loading everything into the hired lorry and then the long, long drive from Sussex.

Driving on through the night, we roared along quiet winding roads through slumbering villages. Suddenly, there were mountains, shadowy in the pale moonlight. We thundered up onto Rannoch Moor, the many lochans reflecting the luminous hazy light and descended down into deep Glencoe. A halt and a stretch was called for and on stopping and opening the door, the silence was tangible. No sirens or traffic; there was just the rustle of wind in the tussocky grass and heather and the distant gurgle of a peaty burn. It was wonderful to be back and this time it was for really for good. I put my head back and savoured the crisp clean air.

There was a blustery dawn rising through ragged clouds as we arrived at last at the port at the end of the longest first leg of our journey. Despite our fatigue, a great feeling of anticipation and excitement surged through us.

Down in the port, the Fisherman's Mission was just opening. It was an oasis of warmth, coffee, bacon and eggs. Sometime later, a walk down onto the pier gave us an idea of what the morning was really like. Huge green waves lashed against the harbour walls and there was even a swell coming into the inner harbour. The wind sighed and moaned in the rigging of the trawlers tied up alongside, as they moved and jostled uneasily together.

As we battled against a blowing gale, a few herring gulls lifted from the pier in front of us and were tossed backward by the fierce wind to land further up the harbour and continue their scavenge for fish offal. Our faces were liberally splashed with a salty spray and we had to shout to each other to be heard. A few people were moving about, but many vessels seemed to be tied up for the day. Not a day for moving furniture in a small boat across the sea.

The plan had been for a friend, James, to come over with his boat and a barge, so we could load everything from the lorry into the barge and tow it up the loch to our new home. The rain then started and we retreated to the warmth of the Mission for endless cups of coffee, moving on somewhat effortlessly later on to one of the pubs for a beer. James arrived around lunchtime. We had known him for several years; he was an intrepid seaman and we were not surprised to see him, having bashed his way against a strong southerly gale into port.

"No way," James announced between sips of frothy beer. "Come back and stay with us tonight and we will see what tomorrow is like."

That day was our first harsh lesson that up here you are ruled by the weather and the tides, not timetables. The lorry would not be back in Sussex the next day. The sea was now far too wild to attempt to move furniture and horizontal rain whipped against the pub windows.

A while later, we clambered down the pier steps and into James' sturdy boat, which was tied at the pier for the journey back to his isolated home. He seemed quite unperturbed by the gigantic swell following us, as we left the shelter of the harbour. I wondered whether it was like this often, feigning nonchalance and trying to carry on a conversation, while out of the corner of my eye I could see huge, green cresting waves threatening to overtake us.

Much later, in the warmth and calm of their solid stone house, the gale still howled up the sound. Fortified by a good meal, we slept soundly as the wind whistled and whined outside and the icy sleet pummelled the skylight in the bedroom roof.

The following day dawned crystal clear and calm; all vestiges of yesterday's storm had vanished as if it had never happened. How could it change so quickly? There were now only small waves cruising past the inlet where the night before a massive swell had thrashed into the headland.

The boat was brought off moorings and the barge lashed alongside it. It was a deep heavy barge some thirty feet long and had taken quite a lot of pushing to launch it off the slip. At one stage, James had waded into the water in his underpants to lever a large rock out of the way.

"When we are out in the sound we will tow it behind," James explained.

Some common seals suddenly bobbed their heads up inquisitively nearby to see what was happening as we worked. I had never seen wild seals so close before and they brazenly watched us through their huge watery eyes.

The voyage back to port was beautiful; the islands well out to sea almost seeming to hover like a mirage above the water. The sky was blackbird egg blue with just a wisp of cloud on the tops of the Cuillin mountains way across the sound on Skye.

Back in the fishing harbour, the barge was pulled alongside again and the boat came in slowly to the pier steps. Every item lifted out of the lorry had to be carried down these steep iron steps and stowed evenly in the barge so that the weight was balanced.

A small group of people gathered to watch and some helped. Our worldly possessions were being well and truly aired in public. We had only brought essentials of furniture with us, some treasured antiques, books and paintings. A huge number of loved items of our past twenty years of life together had been sold or given away. It was obvious that for a couple of years we would only have limited space in the old house.

Eventually, the lorry was empty and the barge and boat full, the last item being a huge floral print sofa that was perched on top of everything else. This seemed like a good place to make my entrance into our new life and I opted to ride down the loch sitting on the sofa in the barge. We waved goodbye to our helpers, who were probably wondering what sort of eccentric English people we were to be going and living right up a remote loch on our own, with no modern amenities.

The boat left harbour and the barge was strung out behind to start the final phase of our journey. What a way to move house. I sat resplendent on our floral sofa like Cleopatra on her golden barge.

"The barge she sat in like a burnished throne." Except that my barge was black steel with rusty bits and my Marc Anthony, somewhat dishevelled, was squashed with our dog, Barney, among packing cases crowded onto the deck of the boat.

We rounded the point, leaving the open sea and started up the loch. The water sparkled and creamed past the blunt bows of my conveyance. I had a wonderful view up the loch, spoilt only by the occasional whiff of diesel fumes percolating back from the boat. As we made our way away from the fishing town, I could just see the cluster of houses off two to three miles to my left. This would be our nearest village, six miles by boat from the house in which we would be living.

The loch changed direction and high hills fell steeply to the water. We passed a ruined settlement sheltered on a hillside, with a tree covered promontory jutting into the calm waters. In the far distance, we could just catch a glimpse of the white house that was to be our new home. We had camped in the old unlocked house some two years previously when foul weather had driven us off the high hills on a walking holiday. Never in our wildest dreams would we ever have believed that we would end up living there. I can still remember Pete saying to me back then, "Would you like to live here?"

"Oh yes," I replied.

The sun felt hot on my face and the odd sea bird rose in front of us. There were guillemots and a shiny black cormorant, looking almost reptilian, was diving just off from the boat. Some ten minutes later, an inlet off to our right led into a tiny sheltered bay with an old house tucked up under crags to the side. This was where our nearest neighbour lived and where we would pick up our mail each week.

Approaching the narrows in the loch, the men hauled the barge by hand alongside the boat and made fast with ropes before attempting to enter the narrow channel of water. Our arrival had been timed so that the tide was neither rushing in or out, a subtle point that hadn't until then occurred to Pete or me. Our learning curve on the nuances of the tide in those narrows would be something learned very quickly in the first few weeks of living there.

The inner loch continued for some six miles and widened out to contain billions of gallons of water, which hurled and fought its tumultuous way in and out through the narrow channel twice every twenty four hours. Many a time in the following years we were to see boats battling against the eight knot maelstrom and sometimes give up to wait for the race to lessen. Today it was still; the tide was out, but would soon turn.

The boat dropped anchor in the bay just below the house and a degree of manoeuvring by hand of the barge, together with a good push provided the heavy craft with enough impetus to glide up onto the steep boulder shore. I was still perched aloft as the men rowed ashore and tied the barge off securely to a stout post at the top of the rocky beach. The tide was starting to turn and flow back in and we would have to work fast to unload. We had roughly six hours before it would start to ebb and then there would be the possibility of the barge being stranded high and dry until the following day.

I took just a minute to sit and absorb the spectacular view of the ultramarine blue water stretching away to the head of the loch encircled by high and dramatic peaks. Nearby, the old stone house stood solid and squat, a large sycamore tree casting shadows onto its walls. It was a wonderful feeling. I felt as if I had come home; a home with no central heating, electricity, phone or road, nor even a footpath to the village. Nobody had lived there for over twenty years.

There was no time to sit and muse; the rising water was already nudging the craft up the beach. We struggled up the slippery seaweed covered rocks with every item. An old tractor and trailer had been recently purchased and brought by landing craft down to "Caolas", the name of our new home. In Gaelic it meant "Where a loch narrowed down to a channel of water".

Each item was loaded into the trailer and, when full, was driven the short way up the steep slope and into the farmyard for the final move into the house. As the tide rose, we had to keep shortening the mooring rope because the barge lifted higher and higher. As compensation for this, the distance that we had to carry furniture and boxes up that lethally slippery, slope was shorter.

I think we both felt that afternoon that once we were established in the house, one of the first jobs would be to clear the seaweed and the bigger boulders and make a safer slip to bring in boats and supplies. We all worked hard and fast and only one load was left on the trailer as the tide started to turn again. The barge was heaved off the rocks before it became firmly beached.

James left for the twelve mile journey back to his home. He would not arrive home before dark. There we were, with our old dog Barney and the last of our "flittings" on a lonely beach, with the tangerine sun setting behind the old house. We stood for a minute in the peace to listen to the calls of some oystercatchers "kleep-kleeping" away around the point in the sandy bay. It was so quiet.

Last load in and we were home. A Rayburn had been fitted prior to our move and we wasted no time finding the bag of coal amongst our possessions. A paraffin Tilley lamp was lit for light in the kitchen and we sat down, exhausted but happy, and ate a simple meal.

The only sound outside was the swirling of the tide as it raced out of the narrows. Not a light of any other habitation, just a large full moon rising over the mountains at the head of the loch. We slept deeply that night and woke the next morning excited and ready to start our new life with all its challenges.

Chapter Two

The New Boat

Pete was annoyed. I knew it by his stance; his clenched fists and the odd oath he muttered. He pressed the engine button on the old boat one more time and the starter whirled. A small amount of white smoke curled lazily from the exhaust, but the engine resolutely refused to start.

"Give me the Easy Start," he said in exasperation. "I hate using that bloody stuff." He was after all a mechanic amongst other qualifications and such substances were an anathema to him.

I had already dug the half empty can out of the locker in anticipation and mutely passed it to him. It was not the moment to make a comment. A well aimed jet of the powerful liquid was squirted at the essential part of the oily innards and the button pressed again. This time, as if by magic, the old engine erupted into life and we were engulfed in a dense pall of black smoke. The drug addicted engine had to have its daily "fix" before it would start.

This was the boat named Penelope, or rather more aptly the Penny Lope, as our Belgium employer pronounced her and she was our only form of transport for the first few weeks at Caolas, until a more suitable boat could be purchased. She was small, long and narrow and really only suitable for inland waterways.

Our new employer realised the importance of a bigger, more seaworthy boat and we were asked to seek expert help in procuring a good, second hand sturdy boat. Copies of "Fishing News" littered the kitchen table with red rings in biro around adverts of likely boats to see. A thirty foot ex-fishing boat looked a possibility and she was for sale some miles down the west coast from us. It was nearly winter and we had no time to waste.

It was time to go and buy a boat.

A rising wind rattled the riggings of the fishing boats as they heaved and banged together against the harbour wall. It was a Saturday night and many boats were tied up having run in before the storm. Over the strong stone pier, a big sea was cresting and crashing onto the rocks below and sending flumes of spray high up the wall. The light marking the dangerous skerries just outside the harbour flashed weakly on and off and the orange glow of the town street lights were reflected in the relatively calm waters within. I called the boat's name twice.

"Calypso, Calypso, do you read?" I said urgently into the portable VHF radio handset. This was the second time that night that I had walked down to the harbour to try and contact the overdue boat. I had driven back up the coast and was waiting for the men, Pete and Murdo, a hired boatman from the village, to come back into town with the newly purchased boat and pick me and the dog up so that we could complete the journey to our remote farmhouse over ten miles further up the loch. The radio stayed resolutely silent; nothing. They should have been back. A shiver went up my back that had nothing to do with the cold wind.

"Are you having problems," a nearby voice called from the darkness. A shadowy figure climbed off the pier ladder leading down to the boats below. I answered that a boat was overdue and that I couldn't raise them on my small handset.

"Come down to my boat and we'll try and get them on my

radio," the man answered. Now I wouldn't normally clamber onto a boat with a strange man at 10 o'clock at night, but I was really worried for the men's safety.

His boat was about 80 foot long with a large wheelhouse packed full of state of the art electronics. He tried calling the VHF channel that I was working on. Again, nothing, and then the coastguard intervened to inform us that this boat was in some mechanical difficulty, but no reliable position had been given. They were trying to get a fix on the craft and there was talk of the lifeboat being launched for a search if the men on board couldn't re-start the engines.

"Right then," said Ken, who was my new acquaintance. "We are going out to try and find them." I had learnt that this poor guy had just come into harbour after ten days' continuous fishing far out at sea and was hoping for a quiet night. All of his crew were away at the disco in town and here I was with a total stranger setting out to sea on a wild and stormy night. We left the safe cocoon of the harbour astern and the orange glowing streetlights. Immediately the big boat started pitching as the south westerly gale hurled huge waves at us.

We made our way over to Sleat point, as given the time at sea, the wind direction and the normal course that the men would have taken, my skipper felt that that would be the area where they would be. He kept trying to call up on the radio but to no avail. We scanned the radar screen to try and locate the missing boat at the back of the point, but nothing showed up, just rocks and tiny islands. Ken turned the boat south towards Ardnamurchan point, the route that the men would have taken up the coast. I briefly studied his strong featured face illuminated in the dim lights of the wheelhouse. His quiet confidence and obvious experience took the edge off my worry.

The lights of the town were now well astern, but way off on our starboard beam Eigg lighthouse flashed its unique signal. All the lights have a different sequence I was told and are marked on the sea charts for that area, enabling one to estimate a rough area of position.

It was becoming rougher and rougher as we neared Ardnamurchan point with its powerful light well off to our port side. The big boat was plunging as we drove into the large swell, sending huge sheets of salty water thundering against the wheelhouse window. I was pleased that I was not feeling sea sick, since it was the biggest sea that I had ever been out in.

What on earth were the men in the smaller boat experiencing in this unyielding sea?

Ken handed me the wheel for a few minutes, a great honour, while he quickly went below and arrived back with two steaming mugs of tea and slices of cake. I had never been in the wheelhouse of such a large boat and I sat in the skipper's padded high chair, surrounded by radar, colour sounders and GPS, a device all these twenty plus years later is quite common in the average family car, but was a wonderful new invention then.

We had no better luck off Ardnamurchan point and it was suggested to the coastguard that we set off a large red parachute flare, which might be seen by the lost boat. The coastguard, with their more powerful radio, had been in contact with the missing boat, but they still could not give a position; they were completely lost. I was informed that there was a procedure whereby all the local coastguards had to be alerted before we could send off the flare. Setting off a red flare is usually only undertaken in an extreme emergency. A little while later we received the orders to proceed.

Ken went outside the wheelhouse, balanced himself expertly on the violently rocking deck and held the flare high above his head.

"Please let them see it," I whispered quietly to myself.

It went up with a terrific whoosh and then all the surrounding, tumultuous sea with high cresting waves was lit by this unearthly pinky red glow. In this incredible display of pyrotechnics, the whole sky around our craft looked scarlet. It seemed to last for minutes, but was probably only seconds before the spent flare faded and the blackness folded heavily around us again.

We waited for the coastguard to make contact with us. Surely the flare would have been seen for miles? When they did, it was to inform us that our flare had not been seen, but that the other boat was setting theirs off. Ken and I stood braced on the deck and strained our eyes into the heavy darkness as the stationary boat wallowed in the deep swell. Nothing; all was in inky blackness and yet what was that? There was just a faint pin prick of light many miles to the north west of us. Unmistakably we saw a flare.

"I knew they couldn't be far from Sleat point," said Ken in exasperation as he turned the boat round and headed back north again. The powerful engines throbbed beneath our feet as we churned our way back up the coast. It was a great relief to have some idea where the smaller boat was. We chatted easily as the big boat ploughed on. Ken told me a bit about his life at sea on a fishing boat and I told him about our remote home and our plans for the future. There was a developing empathy between us, for we both lived hazardous lives.

Now we had an idea where the men were, the tension had lifted.

Nearing the point, the radar that had been set on a large scale, showing a large portion of the local coast, was switched to a radius of only about five miles. It showed a viciously dangerous coastline of skerries and wee islets.

"Some of this area is still uncharted," commented a concerned Ken as we closely scanned the screen. "That looks like a boat shape," he said, pointing to a small shadowy image. The men were in grave danger.

At long last we could raise them on the radio. There was a lot of static and the signal kept breaking up. They had been able to restart the engine, but were completely lost. They had no radar on board to show what a dangerous spot they were in. It was going to be very tricky to guide them out into open water again.

We stayed wallowing about three miles out and Ken began by watching the radar screen to try and plot a course to safety for the small boat. We put all the deck lights on so that eventually they would see us. Painstakingly slowly as Ken kept in radio contact and guided them, the shadowy shape on the radar moved out and past the rocks.

The small boat must have been taking a pounding with the huge swell surging into the bay. There was a palpable fear in their voices, which was unmistakable even over the radio. Almost imperceptibly the tiny shape on the screen turned and manoeuvred past the dangerous skerries. We could only pray that there were not semi submerged rocks that would not show on the radar.

Ken's concentration was absolute. I held onto the bench with trembling hands and watched as he methodically instructed the men which way to steer. How could they have sailed into such a dangerous place and remained unscathed? At long last the boat was in open water and before too long we could see her, a small and vulnerable craft in an uncompromising sea. What a relief.

The boat drew alongside and I waved and called to my

husband. His face was pale and drawn. I could only imagine the terror that they had experienced that night.

"Let's go home," said Ken, his voice whipped away by the wind. It was 3.30am, five hours after we had started the rescue. I was allowed to take the wheel again as more cake and tea was rustled up. Using the radar, we guided the following boat safely around the point and then far ahead we could see the orange glow of the fishing port. It had been a successful rescue. Back in port there was absolute relief all round. I jumped down onto the deck of the small boat and embraced Pete. It was so good to see him and our friend again.

Before Ken turned in for a well earned sleep, I hugged him and thanked him for his act of heroism on such a wild night.

It was to be the start of a long friendship between our families.

Chapter Three

Early Days

Becoming used to living in such a remote location was exciting, hard work and sometimes scary, but never boring. There were the obvious differences from our life down south; the lack of roads, no telephone or electricity and no B&Q store nearby, for example, but we had been employed to fulfil building works and this had to start almost immediately.

Our only communication with the outside world was a battery powered VHF radio, which sat in the corner of the kitchen, but the signal range this reached was very limited. We could chat to fishing boats way out to sea and could reach the office serving the stalking estate of miles of wilderness in the village.

Mary in the office became our daily messenger of news from the village and was always a friendly voice. She also played a very important role in our proposed work as she was able to telephone the nearest building merchants fifty miles away and order building materials to be delivered to the road end, over ten miles from us.

It was also necessary at that time for Pete to travel away frequently for several days at a time to coordinate the huge amount of building materials and transport needed for starting to rebuild the ruined cottage. He would leave on the mail boat from the inlet three miles away across the loch and I would be at Caolas on my own.

Those first few weeks were a time before work really started, so once I had finished unpacking all our possessions in the old house, I had time to explore the surrounding area.

I walked on the beautiful pebbly and sandy beach just around the headland from the house and scuffed up cockles with my feet as they lay buried just below the surface. I saw an otter down among the rocks near the house. It had caught a large fish and was so busy eating it that it did not notice me as I crouched and watched it from behind a large boulder. Of course, I didn't have my camera with me.

It was the time of the rut of the wild red deer and the hills behind echoed with their roars. What a wonderful wild place it was. I would sit outside the old house and listen to their primeval calls high on the mountain behind

Setting out early on a bright October morning, I skirted the flat peat bog between the raised beach ground by the shore and the lowest flanks of the hill. Years ago, past inhabitants of Caolas had cut peat there for their fires and the following spring I intended to do the same. It was still slightly misty on the tops of the hills, but the sun was warm on my face. As I started to climb, a naturally formed terrace took me up at an angle past a patch of Grass of Parnassus with its delicate white flowers. Numerous tiny burns, some merely trickles, crossed my way. Overhead a skein of geese in a V formation were flying south for the winter. They were way up high, but their honking calls transmitted down to me as I climbed. I paused and watched them and wondered where they were bound. Soon I encountered some very rough ground where huge outcrops of schist rock, scoured smooth by glaciers long ago and weather worn for millennia, reared out of the tussocks of grass and heather. The summer green had changed to russets and browns as the bracken and molinia grass died back.

The sound of a large waterfall invaded my ears as I climbed slowly up. A shelter stone marked on the Ordnance map lay ahead. Two massive bus-sized rocks leaned together to create a small cave like shelter, definitely not four star accommodation, but dry and room for one in an emergency. The waterfall fell from the lip of the corrie above and beyond this a ridge high above could possibly be the summit of the mountain.

Above the fall, a huge amphitheatre of a corrie spread out ahead. I stopped suddenly, my eye caught by movement up in the crags. There were deer everywhere; hinds grazing in groups, the colour of their bodies well camouflaged against the mountain.

Then the sound reached me. I had not heard it before for the sound of the waterfall had obscured it; the loud guttural roar of a stag. I crouched behind a rock so that I could not be seen and listened. He was not too far away and I spied him running around a group of hinds as they grazed unconcern-edly. Every few minutes he would open his mouth and let out this guttural bellow, a thrilling spine tingling sound. He was a majestic beast with huge antlers and his muscular body was dark and wet with the mud in which he had wallowed. In this testosterone filled time, stags would coat their bodies to either make themselves look more formidable to other stags or to attract the ladies, but these hinds did not seem impressed. Older stags would roar deeper and with more resonance than young ones.

More stags roared from around the corrie and this orchestra of wild sound mesmerised me. Another large stag suddenly entered the scene from further up the corrie. He sidled around the group of hinds and stood and roared from a knoll. This was a challenge for supremacy not to be ignored. The beast that I had been watching caught sight of this intruder and galloped over to him. There followed a test of wills, where both animals strutted parallel to each other and rolled their eyes in a fero-cious manner. Then they suddenly turned and locked antlers.

First one was pushed backwards and then the other. They were equally matched. This violent scene carried on for several minutes as their antlers were intertwined. One stag had blood on his neck, an injury from an antler. The muscles in their hindquarters rippled as they sparred. The earth was churned up in this frenzy and one of the stags fell to his knees. He was down and fell backwards. It was suddenly over. The intruder picked himself up, turned and raced away over the rough ground chased by the prime stag.

I felt privileged to have witnessed such a scene and skirted around the corrie so as to not disturb the deer as the wind blew my scent away from them. The last haul up to the summit had me puffing and with each step the panorama of the view opened before me. A ptarmigan, now half in its winter white plumage, uttered a noisy staccato protest as it flew away and I scrambled up the final rocky crest to the top.

All the hills that in the years ahead I would get to know from their shapes and positions lay before me. I would eventually climb many of them. I sat and ate my "piece", my map spread out on the ground as I started to learn their names.

October passed and the deer stopped roaring; the rut was over and their passion spent. The hills were silent again.

My times of wandering on the mountains would be limited for some time. We had an enormous job to do and the first load of building materials arrived one day on board a large landing craft. Work on the ruined cottage had started.

Chapter Four

Fetching the Mails

During the first two months of living at Caolas, we didn't have a big boat for putting to sea and getting in supplies. We had to rely on the mail boat dropping food supplies off with our nearest neighbour, Donald, over three miles away across the loch. We would leave a note with him for the skipper of the mail boat to give to the man at the grocery shop the week before we needed the food. They would then leave a box of our groceries with all the other supplies on the pier by the mail boat. It was imperative to send a complete list. If we forgot anything it was tough and we had to manage without it for another week. We were in effect marooned for this time. Luckily, when we first arrived, I had stocked up the larder in the old house with tinned and non perishable food. Tinned ravioli and corned beef can, however, become a bit monotonous.

The newly acquired thirty foot boat, the Calypso, was away in port at the boat yard having engine repairs and modifications after the adventurous voyage home since her purchase and the Penny Lope had sailed on to a new owner.

All we had was a small inflatable dinghy and a strange wooden craft that had been used by its previous owner, James, as a hopper for collecting building sand from a beach. It was supposed to be towed behind a larger boat and was made of wood exterior ply and roughly 10 foot long by 4 foot wide, deep and flat bottomed, with a square stern and sloping prow. It had a sort of open coffin shape, which was rather an uncomfortable thought. We had acquired a small outboard engine, which when clamped firmly to the stern and fully revving, would push this ungainly craft along at about two knots. If you sat well down in the middle to keep the centre of gravity low and were not too fazed by the creaking and flexing of the sides, it provided a calm water "get about".

It was our only way of crossing the narrows at slack tide, to then walk the three miles and collect our mail and food. Using it was not without adventures and one epic crossing nearly ended in disaster.

In the early autumn, when we first came to live at Caolas, the mail boat only came up the loch twice a week on Monday and Friday afternoons. It would sail in to the inlet two miles down the loch from us and drop off mail and goods by dinghy on the rocky shore close to our nearest neighbour's house. There would be anything from coal and bottled gas, food, letters, hikers with incredibly heavy rucksacks, tools and poultry food. Our neighbour Donald would pick up our mail along with his own and keep it for us to collect.

You could almost tell the time on "mail" afternoons by the distinct drumming of the powerful twin Kelvin engines as the boat came into view far down the loch. It was to become a welcome sound later in deep winter when maybe nobody had been up the loch in several days. Even on a wild day when waves would be cresting past the entrance to the inlet and crashing noisily onto the headland, the water within would be sheltered. Sometimes, if it was calm, we would cross the narrows in the ungainly hopper or rubber dinghy and walk the couple of miles to Donald's house and sit with him to wait for the mails, but usually we waited for the tide or the weather to be right and so sometimes our mail was only picked up once a week.

It was a calm October afternoon and the loch was like a satin mill pool, ebony dark and still. We had listened to the shipping forecast at 1.55pm, with crackly hissing reception on the battery powered radio and there was a forecast for bad weather with gales coming in before evening. So far, strong winds all week had thwarted any mail or food collection and neither of us could face another tin of Irish stew.

The tide cycles were also at high springs. This is due to the moon being either full or new; huge rises and falls occur between high and low tide and massive volumes of water racing through the narrows form whirl pools and tumbling eddies. A neap tide the following week would see much smaller rises and falls. A gale and a strong tide was not a good combination for crossing the narrows, especially in the sand hopper, but the dinghy was even smaller. Low tide and slack water was at approximately 3pm, the only time to risk a crossing, if only the promised gale would keep away for a while longer.

We hauled the heavy wooden hopper down the steeply sloping, stony beach. It was much easier since we had cleared most of the tangled weed and larger boulders and in fact we had found remnants of a slip used by the last people to have lived at the house many years ago.

The outboard engine was attached and with a couple of pulls on the starter rope and a punt off from the shore, we were away. The tide was really low and fronds of leathery kelp, normally hidden below the surface, threatened to foul the propellers. The narrows, which had been a boiling maelstrom only three hours before, were now safe and still to cross. We could see sea urchins on the barnacled rocks far below and star fish draped in clusters over boulders.

The crossing at low tide in springs was only about sixty yards across and I was soon stepping out onto the far shore. Pete stayed with the hopper to keep it in the water while I walked to Donald's house and back. There was an old track along the far shore to the inlet, but I knew it would not be too long before the tide turned and would make the return trip over the narrows hazardous. I set off at a trot across the short nibbled turf, liberally scattered with sheep turds, past the shuttered white holiday cottage and then several ruined houses before the track started to climb 'round the headland.

Back in the nineteenth century, there had been quite an inhabited settlement on that side of the narrows, with a school house that the children on the Caolas side of the narrows would attend; weather and tide permitting. They would be rowed across and back each day.

The old track that I was now on was once used to reach the Chapel in the inlet. It was not difficult to visualise men and women in their Sunday black, leaving their homes and clambering up and 'round the headland for the long Sunday services. In places the track was still clear with stone steps, but in others it was now overgrown with thick wiry heather that hindered my quick steps. I was puffing by the time I started dropping down into the bay. The loch was still eerily calm, the mountain sides dark against a flat grey sky.

I went down the old stone steps and through the rusty gateposts and into the inlet. The kelp heads were still nodding above the surface and a heron stood motionless at the water side. I had not long before the tide would turn, but I knew I couldn't just rush into my neighbour's house and grab our mail. That would be too rude when there were always things to talk about; the latest news and gossip to exchange.

Several collie type dogs of different colours erupted out of the open doorway to announce my arrival.

"Come in, come in!" a voice called from the dark interior. "Sit you down and just get your breath."

The kettle had already been moved to the hotplate of the old black stove as I breathlessly dropped onto the old settee by the window. The dogs crowded around me with passionate licks to any bare flesh. Jessie, Donald's sister, went into the back scullery for biscuits and cake. They had lived in that old house for most of their long lives and Jessie had been born in a croft house only three miles down the loch. In spite of living in this remote location and the fact that Donald's last trip to Glasgow had been some years back, they were both articulate and very knowledgeable about current world affairs. Like us, a battery radio kept them up to date. Often on my mail trips Donald would converse in depth on some current crisis, bringing his own wisdom to the often intangible events of the "civilised" world a million miles away from this quiet secluded backwater. I sensed a discussion brewing with the tea that afternoon, but quickly quaffed my drink and cake and made a hasty exit. Donald understood. He had also heard the shipping forecast and he was wiser to the ways of the weather and tides than I would ever be.

Up the old stone steps, retracing my footsteps over the headland while clutching a bag of letters, I ran on, my rucksack bouncing and heavy with groceries. A sudden breeze riffled my hair, then another; the oily darkness of the water below now disturbed. Way down the loch to the west a wind was suddenly forced down off the high hills and blasted onto the surface of the loch, a swirl of turbulence picking up a spiral of water and racing it across the surface. The tide had turned and the kelp heads were once more submerged. I had to hurry as the storm was fast approaching.

The wind was much stronger as I reached the shore again and there were now steep sided waves in the narrows with white crests like whipped eggs. Pete and the hopper were higher up the beach and with the tide starting to flow in faster and the wind rising, he was having to battle to stop the waves battering the old craft on the rocks. It was going to be difficult to get the hopper facing out into the narrows, push off and get the outboard going before being thrown back onto the beach.

The wind was screaming now in the narrows and the first heavy drops of rain soused our faces. We tried several times to push off, only to have a wave nearly swamp the stern and lift and hurl the craft back to shore. We knew the longer we left launching, the worse it would become and we would be in real danger. What were our options?

Only two hundred yards or so, over the narrows in the growing gloom, a large candle shone out from our kitchen window, which we had lit before we left to guide us home. There would be peace and warmth by the Rayburn and Barney would be sprawled out on his bed, stretching in his sleep, awaiting his supper.

One alternative was to tie the hopper to a post on the beach where it would probably be wrecked in the night, walk back to Donald's house and impose on his hospitality until the morning or whenever the storm abated. The other totally impractical alternative was to leave the hopper and walk the six miles down the pathless south side of the loch to the head, cross a dangerous river and walk six miles back up the pathless north shore to our home. It was not an option in the failing light. No, we had to get over the narrows and we had to go immediately.

The tide was rapidly increasing in volume and valuable time had already been wasted in futile attempts to launch. Increasingly desperate, wet and miserable, we waded again into the crashing waves and pushed as hard as we could. The cold water surged against my thighs and the boat slammed into my ribs. Pete jumped in and pulled on the starter rope and the cantankerous old engine started first pull; what a blessed sound! The boat was clear and I clambered over the sloping prow and crouched as low as I could. Pete turned into the churning narrows, the little engine screaming and faltering in quick succession as we wallowed over crests and plunged through corkscrewing whirlpools. Big waves and troughs raced past us, the current carrying us rapidly up past our landing spot, the light of the house receding further and further astern.

I shivered with cold and fear as the hopper creaked and flexed alarmingly. It was not made for that kind of sea. We would lurch forward on a wave and drop sickeningly into a trough as that wave would race on to crash eventually on the shore at the head of the loch six miles away. I baled as fast as I could with an old saucepan, while Pete kept the engine revving and guided us across. The far rocky beach was now nearer and we were at last out of the main tide race. The danger was over, even if we did land some five hundred yards further up the loch from our normal spot.

We were safe. We hugged each other, tied the hopper to a big boulder at the top of the beach and made for home, the sea water dripping out of the bottom of the food rucksack; that would be the sugar ruined. Never was a warm kitchen so welcome, the big candle still burning brightly on the window-sill and the storm outside so distant now. Our dear dog rose stiffly from his bed and greeted us with licks on our salty faces. It all seemed so normal later, sitting by the Rayburn dry and warm again and opening a week's worth of mail, even if it was rather wet mail. Precious letters from friends and grocery bills were placed on the Rayburn rail to drip dry.

One letter was from friends down south who, on the day of writing, had been stuck for ages in a six mile traffic jam on the M25. Another world!

Chapter Five

What? No Signal

How easy it is nowadays. Instant communication by phone is something that we take for granted; even Polar explorers can ring home. A mobile phone will still not work at Caolas, because it is cradled by high hills, with no sight of human habitation.

Living at Caolas was as though someone had taken a knife and sliced away the modern world. We could talk on our VHF radio to fishing boats way out to sea, as long as we occasionally took the battery up to the village to recharge it. Enquiries had been sought about the possibility of installing a phone, but British Telecom, not known for philanthropy, quoted an awesome figure to lay a cable over eight miles up hill and down glen, so we refused their offer.

Despite living in a nineteenth century house, we were employed by an employer in a very twentieth century city office who needed fairly frequent progress updates. One day we received a radio message from the village saying that he wished to talk to us on the telephone and could we ring him the following Tuesday morning at ten. This appointment with the modern world, however, posed certain difficulties as the big boat was still away undergoing repairs and we had no way other than walking to reach the village. This would entail trekking about eight miles of trackless hillside, make the calling and walking back, which was not possible on a short November day. It would have to be a two day expedition.

As we set off on the Monday morning, the luxuriant summer growth on the flat meadow had long since turned to russets and browns. The weather was dull and flat with hardly a whisper of a breeze. On a fine morning, the sun would just rise above the opposite hills, but today it was a sepia day. The first small climb of the day spurred the muscles into action and took us over the rocky promontory rising abruptly at the end of the flat meadow. At one time there must have been a path around or over this spur and into the next bay, a horseshoe shaped bay, where in the future I would lay my fishing net and I would often come to watch an otter family. A peaty burn cascaded vertically down from a corrie above and gurgled through what historically must have been grazing ground. A lichen and moss- festooned rickle of stones suggested an old sheep fank with a wall running down to the shore. The first storms of winter had washed sea detritus high onto the rocky shore, with tangled stems of kelp piled high as if heaped there by a huge machine, but this was the power of the sea.

We pushed on past the remains of an old jetty, which had served the abandoned Mica mine high in the hills behind. Once men and ponies had worked here, bringing the mica down the mountainside where it was shipped out by sea from this jetty.

Further up the coast, we walked to a spot where we had camped a couple of years earlier. It brought back memories of a good holiday in the hills. In the spring when we had camped there, warblers sang their sweet song from the branches of the old oak trees and pipits ascended on fluttering wings to then descend again, calling their piping song.

I had heard my first snipe drumming from that place. It was early morning and I thought I heard a goat bleating outside the tent. Upon unzipping the tent door and looking out, I couldn't see anything and snuggled down in my bag again. Maddeningly, the noise started again just as I got comfortable and I hauled myself up to look out for the second time. I couldn't see this pesky goat and was just about to descend into my warm bag again when there it was, a snipe diving earthwards and making this strange sound as the air riffled through its tail feathers.

There were no birds there that November day and the only sounds that could be heard where the ones that we made as we tramped through the dead crackling bracken that sprawled across the ground.

Out over the next promontory and looking back, we could still see Caolas an hour's tramp behind. The next section was very rough and there wasn't even a memory of a path. The hills fell at an unrelenting angle from the long abandoned summer sheilings high above and down to the sea. There was no way of walking along the shore, as sheer buttresses fell into the loch. To make matters worse, there were three parallel burns that had to be crossed and these were swollen by heavy overnight rain. I already had a wet leg from a misjudged leap over the burn in the horseshoe bay with my heavy rucksack on my back. The three were crossed without mishap, just wet legs and a very wet dog shaking pints of water over us.

We sighed with relief after this point as we were over halfway and the bonus was that we could angle down over a huge, smooth glacier-scoured whalebone of rock onto the shore. To stride along with hands in pockets on wiry turf above the high tide mark was easy and we were soon nearing the final climb of the day.

We knew from previous experience that once this had been

ascended, we would finally see the village in the distance still some two miles away. It was not long before we passed the farm and were on a proper road for the last mile. As we trudged the last bit, I was thinking to myself that after all this effort I hoped that our boss would be in his office the following morning.

True to Highland hospitality, as soon as we were seen entering the village, we were immediately offered a warm place in a living room to lay our sleeping bags for the night. Almost as an aside it was added that there was going to be a bit of a get together at that house that night. Now evening "get togethers" have the habit of going on well into the night and this did not sound like an exception to the norm. It would be good to see well known faces from our years of holidaying in the area and folk we hadn't seen since moving into Caolas.

The population of the tiny village had been somewhat expanded by a gang of six burly building workers from Devon doing construction work on a property nearby. They soon arrived in the living room laden with carry outs; carrier bags full of beer and whisky. The small room steadily filled and the atmosphere was jovial. Now and again the door would open and a cool breeze would waft in as more people squeezed into the room.

The conversation was about the lamb sales, the recent gales, poor Douglas's boat that had broken its mooring and got wrecked in the last storm, and the bull that had been with the cows all summer, yet not one was pregnant. Several people had their own earthy ideas on that one.

"Firing blanks," growled Johnny to no one in particular.

The drams flowed and the evening passed in a warm haze. Our dog snoozed gently by my side and my eyes were heavy. At some point during the party, Pete and I fell asleep comfortably sprawled on the large sofa. It was not entirely down to alcohol, but exhaustion after our long walk.

Just as the first dull November light was filtering through the curtains the next morning, I was awoken by strange snoring. I knew Pete could snore expansively and Barney had his moments, but this was a different noise; rhythmic and exceedingly loud with gurgling noises on the exhalation. The whole room seemed to vibrate to this ululation. I rubbed my eyes and focused on the source of this dreadful noise, which was very close to me. It was then that I saw shadowy shapes dotted on various chairs around the room and the fearsome snoring was right next to me.

That was an awful moment of realisation; I had spent the night sleeping with the six builders from Devon. I hastily made sure that Pete was still on the sofa next to me.

Oh dear, this was the phone call morning and I sat outside on the doorstep very tired and maybe just a little hung over. Even the old dog looked morose.

Later from the tiny office, we dialled the direct number to Belgium. I imagined our employer wearing a finely cut suit sitting in a lovely heated office somewhere in Brussels and surrounded by fax machines, computers and secretaries. His voice answered from another world.

"Yes, we are feeling fine," we said and told him that the rebuilding of the cottage had commenced.

He rang us back and we both talked with him for some time. I could hear the roar of city traffic behind his voice and a siren wailing somewhere.

My eyes glanced up through the window and I saw a small boat bobbing gently at its mooring in the bay, as some gulls wheeled noisily over the pier. In the distance across the loch, majestic dark hills marched away into the distance.

A ramshackle blue pickup truck pulled up outside and six weary workers climbed unsteadily into the back before it roared away in a cloud of blue smoke. All was quiet again and a tabby cat sat licking itself in the middle of the road. I knew where I would rather be.

Yes, we did make the eight miles back to Caolas before dark.

Chapter Six

Hard Lessons about Moorings

Because of its situation on a point, Caolas was buffeted by all winds. We would learn about the early spring winds that would scream down the loch from the east, picking up force as they howled into the narrows, causing the waves to gain height the further they rolled down the loch. The term for this was 'the fetch' on the waves and by the time they flung themselves through the narrows and onto the shingle point, the fetch would be spectacular, especially on a high spring tide. Dry and sunny April days, which were blasted by a searing cold easterly wind at Caolas, would be warm and balmy at the sheltered village. The south and west winds were always the most ferocious. Often, they would start from an oily calm on the loch and then attain their full fury within an hour.

It was such an afternoon in November when we experienced the elements hurling everything at the old house. At first, the branches on the large sycamore tree outside began to bow and sway. Sudden little whirlpools far down the loch whipped up the water into spouts that weaved and raced up the loch and the next minute all the old windows rattled. The slates on the roof started to ripple from one end to the other like a Mexican wave at a sports' event. During the peak of the storm the house juddered, even with three foot thick walls. On opening the door into the yard, the handle was almost ripped out of my hand and the winds had created a sort of vacuum in the enclosed space where it was difficult to catch your breath.

That afternoon we watched buckets being hurled away from the back door and a piece of loose tin take off spectacularly and fly like a kite over the byre roof. All this time we were worried about the boat at moorings. It was only a week since the boat had come back from the boatyard after many repairs and a brand new mooring had been laid by a local man in the next bay up the loch from the house. We would like to have had a mooring outside the house in the bay, but this was deemed too difficult and dangerous, given the eight knot tide race that swirled and thundered every day through the narrows, so the mooring was laid out of the racing waters in a quiet bay nearly a mile away up the loch and out of sight.

This gale was particularly fierce and we knew we could do nothing about the boat, but we felt we had to check that it was alright. Huge waves were rolling past in the narrows and a few herons were sheltering, hunched up, in the shingle spit as we left the warm kitchen and made our way out of the yard and into the open. It was difficult to stand and sudden blasts would send us to our knees. We dropped down to the beach to try and obtain some shelter and made our way to the promontory, which we had to cross to reach the next bay. Pete held my hand tightly as gusts and lashing rain threatened to send us spinning. Over the top of the promontory, we crawled on hands and knees. It was impossible to speak as words were whipped away. The wind screamed in our ears.

I'm not sure if the emotion that hit us first was disbelief or horror, or both, as we crested the rise and looked into the bay. There was no boat, nothing; no pink mooring buoy, just creaming waves. We had both told each other on the way to the mooring that surely the boat would be fine and I think we believed this until we looked down into the bay. We just hung there together in that raging storm with our mouths open. Where was it? It was our lifeline. No boat meant an awful long way to walk out. We tried to scan the coastline through the murk, but the wind and the lashing horizontal rain obliterated everything.

I'm not sure how long we crouched there in shock, almost unaware of the fury around us, before we realised that there was nothing that we could do that night. The precious boat was gone, probably smashed to bits on the various skerries and promontories between us and the head of the loch. Battling back to the house against the gale was even worse and we were already soaked to the skin, even through good water-proofs. The force of the wind took our breath away and hurt our lungs and the biting, stinging sleet was like hundreds of wee needles assaulting our faces. The warmth of the kitchen was bliss as we shut the door on the fury outside.

After a restless night, dawn came in with an eerie silence. The wind had veered to the north and it was much colder, but almost calm. At that time, our only other boats consisted of a tiny rubber dinghy, sufficient to row out from the shore of the bay to the big boat, and the wooden sand hopper in which we had already had adventures fetching the mail. There was nothing for it but to put the outboard on the back of the hopper and head up the loch to search for the wreckage. It was slow work with only a four horse powered outboard engine pushing the ungainly craft at two to three knots. Pete urged the hopper on up the loch side as I scoured the shoreline with binoculars right up to the head of the loch where the high mountains fall steeply down to a wide sandy bay. At any moment we expected to see bits of wreckage and had become quite philosophical, but very sad about the loss of the boat. How would we explain this latest saga of the boat to our boss?

Now and again, vicious heavy squalls would beat down on us and I would bail out the hopper. Then, miraculously, the sun would suddenly return from behind retreating dark cloud masses, lighting up the surrounding hills in pale colours. The many waterfalls, still milky white from the torrential rain the night before, thundered down off the surrounding hills into the loch.

I spied something through the binoculars far away at the head of the loch that was not normally there. There were no huge rocks on the sandy beach there, but there was definitely something far up on the sand; a shape very much like a boat.

"There she is!" I shouted above the noise of the engine. There would be no other boat down there.

We gradually drew nearer and there was the wonderful boat beached on the smooth white sand and lying way out in front of it was the concrete mooring block, buoy and chain. She was intact, not damaged at all. It was unbelievable that she had sailed off at the height of the storm, dragging the heavy mooring, missing all the rocks on the way and landing safely on a sandy beach.

All that we could do was to tie the hopper off and wait on her deck for the tide to come in so that we could float off again. We were hungry by now and the day was cold. Heavy sleet showers still raced across the loch and we suddenly noticed as clouds cleared that the high tops of the mountains were dusted in a sprinkling of snow, the first of that winter. In between the showers bright sunlight danced on wavelets sweeping diagonally across the loch.

We waited and pondered as to what we could do with the boat, for we now had no mooring at home for her. The nearest safe mooring with a flat sea bed was three miles from the house at the inlet where we picked up our mail, so this was where we decided to go. We could drop the mooring buoy in the bay there and leave the boat until we arranged a safer mooring at Caolas.

The water had started to rise around the boat and as she started to float we pulled the long heavy chain onboard until we were floating right by the concrete mooring. Dumping the large pink float and quantities of chain on the deck, we secured the mooring alongside with ropes. We would have to sail back up the loch towing the heavy weight with us. As she rose, she took on a considerable list to starboard where all the weight was and eventually we were properly afloat. It was good to start up the engine and move back down the loch slowly, albeit a bit lopsided.

Sometime later and close to dark, we sailed slowly into the inlet, cut the ropes and dropped the mooring in the sheltered bay, leaving the boat bobbing upright again in a safe place for the time being.

For a week or so, we left the boat where she was and used the hopper to get about. During this time we ordered by radio, via a friend in the village, a longer length of heavy chain from the chandler in the fishing port. Another friend, who was much more knowledgeable about moorings, heard about our dilemma on the radio and came down to see us, bringing various shackles and a heavy metal eyelet to cast on top of the new mooring block. He threw light on what had probably happened to the first mooring. In his opinion, the mooring chain had been too short, causing the boat to snatch up and down at the block. The key to a good mooring was in having a good length of really heavy chain on the bottom, which acted like a spring and allowed the boat to ride up and down in any sea. The first mooring had been laid on a steeply sloping seabed with too short a rising chain and as the boat had lurched up and down in the gale, it had lifted the block each time and dropped it in slightly deeper water until the boat and mooring floated away.

We were very grateful for his advice and it was a hard lesson well learnt. I think we felt very inadequate at this time for everyone seemed to know so much more about all things nautical than we did. It was time for us to begin learning.

We cast a new, larger concrete block on the beach below the house and attached the longer, heavier chain and buoy. Following advice, we decided to lay this mooring in the narrows outside the house and we had been watching the tide to see where the quietest place would be. The only job now was to get the three tons or so of block and chain off the beach and into place. Luckily, we knew someone with a flat barge ideal for attempting this and a couple of radio calls secured the use of this for a few days. The ancient JCB, which we had brought in on the landing craft when the building materials arrived, was to be put to use. It half lifted and shoved the weight to the bottom of the stony beach and we waited for the day when the tide was right to do the job. We had been advised by various people how to proceed as we had never attempted anything like this before.

The morning of the start of the highest tides for a fortnight dawned late and dreary, with the loch mirror calm. We had been up until midnight the night before to hear the shipping forecast on the hissing, crackly, portable radio. The signal was so bad there that we could only pick up snippets, but agonisingly, as the weather forecaster talked his way up the Irish sea and came to Malin and Hebrides, he reported that a force eight or nine was predicted. This was not looking good for laying the mooring and we would possibly have to put off any attempt for another fortnight, until the tides were right again. However, by mid morning, it was still calm. The barge was moored just off the beach with a small anchor and with ropes tying it to the shore.

The water started to creep 'round the concrete block with all the chain and pink float coiled on top. The weather was holding and we decided to go for it. Pulling the barge inshore until it bunted against the block, we waited for the tide to rise. When it did, we were able to manoeuvre the floating heavy flat platform on top of the block and tie it off to the shore. Then, by standing on the deck, we hauled the float and most of the chain onboard. The idea was that once the barge was really floating and the chain was aboard and tied off securely, the rising tide would lift the weight off the beach and we could move out into the bay. This was the theory that had been patiently explained to us. The short length of chain running from the deck to the weight below became very taut as the water rose and I prayed that the strong rope securing it to the barge would hold. It creaked and groaned and the barge sat lower and lower in the water as she took the weight.

Time passed and we wondered if the water would rise far enough to float us before the tide turned. The incoming tide in the narrows beyond us was boiling and swirling with over-falls and whirlpools, for it was about half tide and the time of the strongest surge of water. A long rope secured the barge to the heavy gatepost set above to shore to stop us drifting too far out and to enable us to get back to the shore once the mooring was set.

We waited and waited and the craft took the strain. It was a strong barge and quite capable of carrying that weight. Then, suddenly, the magic moment arrived when we felt a bumping motion and we realised the whole thing was afloat. We knew exactly where we needed to be to drop the mooring and we used long poles to push ourselves hard from the shore. Gently floating out into the bay, we came to the place where the house, the gatepost and the cottage on the other side of the loch were in perfect triangulation, the place we had chosen for the mooring, being out of the worst of the tide race. The tide was nearly in now and had quietened from the boiling maelstrom to a gentle current. We were in place and I stood clear of the chain, as Pete hacked with all his strength at the securing rope with an axe. The final strands parted with a loud crack and the barge shot upwards nearly unbalancing us. The chain flew over the side like a long snake, writhing and twisting, with a terrible grating noise off the deck, followed by the buoy. Then all was still. We had succeeded; the mooring was laid, the pink buoy bobbed quietly in the bay and we were drifting slowly away.

It was then that the first flurries of wind blew through our hair and little wavelets scudded against the barge. The gods had certainly been with us that day and we pulled the craft onto the shore. By the time we had secured it with ropes the wind was beginning to scream and moan up the loch. We had only just completed the job in time.

That mooring came to secure some very heavy boats in the years to come and never let us down.

Chapter Seven

Ladies Aboard

When we first had the new boat, the Calypso, her propensity for breaking down never failed to surprise us. It was becoming apparent that there was still quite a lot wrong with her. In fact, one person renamed her the "Collapso". These malfunctions usually manifested themselves at the most inopportune moments, like rounding the point into port in a gale when, embarrassingly, we had to accept a tow from the mail boat and everyone on the pier was watching. It also happened in the narrow channel at Caolas during a strong tide and well out of radio contact.

The demons under the old rubber mats on the deck were having a laugh again that morning. This time it was the gear box. We were on our way down the loch to fetch supplies, when suddenly our forward motion became erratic. One minute all was well and we were creaming through the water at around eight knots and then we dropped to only a couple. What was also worrying was that the boat would not go into neutral or reverse, which would make life very interesting when we wanted to stop.

Pete removed the matting and the smell of hot oil coming from the gear box was overpowering. He undid the nut on top of the gear box to check the oil level and leapt backwards as a spout of pressurised hot oil shot up in the air like a newly tapped oil well and splattered around the deck with the consistency and colour of crude. Something was definitely amiss in the mechanical innards and, as usual, we were right in the middle of the loch and out of radio signal range. Luckily it was a calm day and with no imminent rocks looming we continued slowly and agonisingly forward.

Our painfully slow progress across the bay in front of the village must have been spotted by sharp eyes ashore and the boat radio hissed, crackled and burbled into life. It always sounded as though the voice at the other end was talking from the bottom of an aquarium. The voice bubbled and faded, but the gist of the call was asking whether we were off into town and could we give some people a lift. It was not mail boat day and folk were obviously stranded.

"Damn," I thought. "The boat is playing up and will not stop and they want us to pick up passengers."

"OK," I replied wearily, not wanting to seem parsimonious. "We are on our way."

As we drew closer, we could see a group of figures on the pier head. The only way to safely come into the pier was across the end in case I couldn't stop. Having shown an aptitude for it, I had taken on the role of skipper since the big boat had arrived. It was a job that Pete had willingly relinquished. So it was up to me to not crash into the pier. To come in down the side of the pier to the steps would be inviting disaster; there being no reverse to stop the boat. Unfortunately, there was only a barnacle encrusted vertical metal ladder off the end of the pier and any passengers wanting a lift would have to clamber down this into the boat.

The wind was picking up and a swell surged around the concrete piles of the pier. Not a good place to try and tie up. We slowly circled near the pier as I shouted ashore and informed the waiting group what the trouble was and what I intended to do. Drawing slowly alongside, someone caught the thrown rope and I pulled the engine stop button.

I bumped somewhat harder than I would have liked against the pier and the rope took the strain, but we had stopped.

We looked up at the small group of people above us and noticed immediately that among the group of anoraks, wellies and tweeds, there were two women in miniskirts and high heels.

"That's odd," I mused. It was a chilly winter day and they were very skimpily dressed. I wondered who they had been visiting as they were obviously not over for the hiking. It became obvious that they were the intended passengers as they clambered gingerly down the old iron ladder, difficult enough to do in boots let alone high heels and miniscule skirts. I was glad to see Pete avert his eyes from his position at the foot of the ladder; there was rather a long expanse of stockinged thigh on display!

There was the usual passing of news between us and the group on the pier and someone passed an empty gas cylinder down for us to get a refill in port and deliver back at some point. It was obvious that we would be having another trip into the boatyard and so might not get back that night.

The two women squeezed into the wheelhouse with me and the dog. One was vigorously masticating gum and the other one immediately lit up a cigarette with scarlet nailed fingers. Not the normal run of the mill for that remote place, but it takes all sorts, I thought, non-too graciously as we headed slowly away from the village. They seemed amiable enough with strong Glasgow accents and loud laughs and by about the eighth cigarette we were slowly nearing the port. There was a distinct fug of smoke and the heady scent of cheap perfume in the wheelhouse.

I had told the two ladies about the trouble with the gear box and that when we got into town I wouldn't be able to come into the usual steps for them to climb up onto the pier, because the harbour shore was only several yards away. I explained that I would have to come alongside the other tied up boats and that they would have to climb over these boats and up another vertical ladder onto the pier. This information didn't go down too well. We were glad the journey was over, because the gear box was incredibly hot and likely to seize at any moment and the sooner we could get the men at the boat yard to look at it the better.

We came alongside the line of tied boats and Pete jumped onto the deck of the nearest one and quickly made fast the rope. I pulled the stop button, but infuriatingly it wouldn't pull out. I pulled and pulled and we started towing all the boats in a graceful arc around the harbour. Eventually the button popped out and we stopped in an untidy heap.

Our passengers were not impressed at the number of boat decks they would have to cross to get to the pier, but I sighed with relief that we were in port. We helped them on their way and once up on the harbour they thanked us and, with bums waggling under tight skirts, they tottered their way towards the railway station.

"Well, that was an experience," Pete commented gruffly. I wasn't sure whether he was referring to the dilemma with the boat, or our two hitchhikers.

Later, from the phone box in town, I rang the pub in the village. I knew by now an assembly of locals would be in for afternoon, pre-supper drinks.

"Who the hell were those two?" I asked. There was first a snigger and then loud laughter and whoops at the other end.

"Don't you know?" There was more communal laughter. It dawned on me at that moment that we had somehow been participants in a larger story and the whole village were enjoying themselves immensely at our expense.

"The building workers from Devon picked up and brought back two prostitutes from their weekend in Glasgow," Jim demurred, before guffawing loudly down the phone.

"You buggers," I gasped.

"Well, we had to get them off the place; there was no work getting done." The mirth was ill concealed.

It was just our luck to be sailing past. Of course, by now the whole of the port would know that the Caolas boat had come down the loch to town and ferried back two Glasgow tarts. Come to think of it, we did get some funny looks.

Chapter Eight

Work and Play

A brisk wind whipped up frothy waves onto the shore. There was a chill in the air for it was now early December. The bare branches of the old sycamore tree rattled together near the house. The days were so short and working time was much less. We had removed the broken slate remains of a roof on the old cottage and dug a pit with the JCB. Rusty corrugated iron, rotten beams, quantities of old wire and fencing posts that had over the years lain in the long grass were shovelled into the hole.

Years of accumulated sheep dung on the floor of the cottage were dug out by hand, loaded onto a trailer and dumped where we planned a vegetable garden. The cottage was ready for renovation and we took the JCB on the sandy shore to load up the trailer with sand to make cement. This had to be accomplished while the tide was out and we hoped that the digger didn't get bogged in the soft sand and then flooded on the next tide.

We had waited some weeks for building permission and a building warrant to be granted. Yes, even in that remote location these rules applied. As two bedrooms were planned upstairs, we would need to extend the walls and gable ends up one and a half metres higher before building a new roof.

All materials had to come in by boat and Pete had spent some time away during that first Autumn organising a huge amount of timber, blocks, plumbing parts, a septic tank and windows, to name but a few. These were all transported from the nearest builder's merchant fifty odd miles away to the fishing port by road and then we hired a large landing craft to move all the material up the loch and onto the beach at Caolas. It had been a hard day's work back at the end of October, but we had a lot of helpers from the village, which made the job easier. I seemed to spend the day making filled buns and cups of tea.

By January we had completed the difficult task of knocking a hole through the thick stone back wall to allow a doorway into what would become a kitchen. The walls were built up and it was time to lay the large concrete slab for the extension. Now, normally one would hire a lorry load of pre-cast concrete for this large area, but of course it was not possible there, so we had to mix it ourselves. The cement was ordered by radioing someone in the village who phoned the merchants. Two tons of cement was due at the port the following Friday and we would use sand from the beach.

That day was calm and fine, although the sun only just peeped over the hill tops opposite. We had lost the sun completely for the fortnight from mid December until early January behind the high hills on the south side of the narrows and it was good to feel it on our faces again.

Once in port, we tied up and waited patiently for the lorry. The days were so short that by 3pm we rang up the merchant, only to discover that the lorry was not coming that day, because the driver was sick. It was so frustrating as the boat journey took an hour and a half each way. It was dark by the time we got back to moorings and with only a torch to light the bay, it was difficult to pick up the buoy in the tide race. What a wasted day. It would be another week before the lorry would come and this was holding up the work.

The following Friday was wet and windy, not an ideal day to collect bags of cement. The building merchants arrived at the road end this time and we manhandled all the bags off the lorry, down the iron steps of the pier and onto a couple of pallets on the deck of the boat. The rain was oozing down our necks. We covered the load with a heavy tarpaulin and lashed it down. Some of the bags were already quite damp.

The boat started rocking as soon as we left port, with water sloshing in and out the scuppers and around the base of the pallet. Up the loch it gradually became calmer, but the rain was still hammering down on the tarpaulin. Once back on moorings, we had to lift every bag from the deck of the boat into the hopper to transport them to the shore, then manhandle them all again into the trailer to get them off the beach and then again into the byre. Inevitably some of the bags became sodden and split apart. I tell you this little story because it illustrates some of the hazards of trying to build a house in such a remote location. Every nut and bolt, toilet seat, door handle and tap had to be brought in by boat and if you forgot to order anything then the job would be held up.

We worked on with hardly a break during that first winter and the weather in January was surprisingly calm and fine. There was still a long way to go, but by spring we hoped to start on the roof. The days were lengthening and the sun was climbing higher in the sky each day.

How good it was to wake to a clear sky with the promise of sunshine when it ventured above the hills. The snow was right down to sea level. Only the bladder wrack on the shore, exposed by the retreating tide, showed any colour. The hills behind were completely covered in a white blanket.

It was a day for walking, not staying at home. I packed my 'piece' for lunch, extra clothing and waterproofs. These were more for a barrier against the cold wind than in anticipation of rain, although conditions there could change rapidly, especially high in the hills. My camera was loaded with a new film and I was ready.

The old house still lay in deep gloom as I left the yard. Two snow buntings crouched on the apex of the barn roof, the first I had ever seen. The frozen snow crunched beneath my boots as I headed out across the meadow by the loch. The south east facing flanks of the high hills were bathed in morning sunlight and glistening white against the blue sky. The birch trees running down to the loch below the hills took on an almost maroon hue.

I left the loch side and started climbing through these woods in a silent world. Weeks of rain had left the ground sodden and where water had trickled the day before, frozen stalactites hung from the banks of the burn. Suddenly, as I ascended, the sun burst over the hill opposite and all was bathed in a brilliant light. I made my way slowly upwards, this pristine whiteness only disturbed by deer tracks, the larger ones from the adults and some smaller ones from their calves, now nearly nine-months-old. There was the single track of a foraging fox on his quest for food or maybe a mate, for this was the courting time for the hill fox. I had hoped to see siskins in the wood and hear their twittering, but no luck that day. I was more likely to see them near the pine woods up at the village. I did see cheerful little chaffinches flitting amongst the scrubby birches where the oak and birch wood thinned.

By now, the snow was up to my knees and I was glad I had not brought the old dog with me, for he would have struggled in the deep snow. With every step I was breaking new ground, for the snow had only fallen in the night and there had been no frosts to consolidate it.

Breaking out onto the open hill high above the wood, the

views were spectacular. I could see right up to the head of the loch, where the serried ranks of high mountains disappeared into the distance. Across the water, I could see over the hills and into the next valley with its deep fresh water loch. Down below me, the house and the cottage were still in the gloom and the sea loch looked dark and still. The sun would be touching the house later in the day and maybe the snow coating the roof of the old house would melt before I got back. I could see the cottage below and the red tractor and yellow JCB looked like tiny matchbox toys. The sunlight was quite intense and almost hurt the eyes. There were no tracks up there and I made my way carefully up the hillside. Once I stepped forward onto a beautiful smooth piece of virgin snow, only to disappear up to my waist. The snow was deeper than I expected and all thoughts of reaching the summit of the mountain were abandoned the further up I went. I decided to reach one of my favourite corries and there I would rest and eat my lunch. I was down to shirtsleeves as the beautiful sun beat down on me from a cloudless sky. It was so quiet; even the wind had dropped.

After another half an hour or so of floundering through the deep snow, I reached the lip of the corrie where the water tips over the edge and rushes down in little pools. It is a lovely spot and I cleared the snow from a large boulder to sit down. All the icicle stalactites hanging from the sides of the burn were dripping from their ends and as I sat some broke off completely to be carried away in the current. I broke one off and sucked it like a lollypop.

I didn't see any deer in the corrie that day. "The white shepherd" as the hill men called the snow, had meant that the beasts had dropped down into the woodland for shelter. I sat there for some time and took in the magnificent vista.

Jumbled white hills became faint blue as they faded into the distance. I arranged my map on the snow in front of me and looked up their names. Some were old friends that I had climbed, but some were unknown to me to explore in the future.

After a while, I gave an involuntary shudder; the wind was picking up and it was getting cold. The day was moving on and I had a long trek back to the house. Dropping down into the woodland again, I heard birdsong once more and the hazel trees with their brave catkins defiantly proclaimed that spring was not far away. What a wonderful and magical day it had been and all the more special because the wind veered by nightfall and warmer south westerlies brought more heavy rain and gales. That meant that within a couple of days all the snow had gone, except from the peaks of the highest mountains.

Chapter Nine

Cutting the Peats

There is a large peat "hag" at the back of Caolas, which many years ago had obviously been used regularly by the people living there to provide fuel for the house fires. Square areas of the moor had been dug away to expose the peat, but over the years since the people left, these were now clothed in heather and sedges again. Inky black, deep, peaty pools dotted the area and sphagnum moss hid some boggy areas from the unwary.

Traditionally, peat cutting always began as soon as the spring weather had dried the moor, usually mid April to the end of May. Quite often dry, easterly winds would blow for days and the tussocks in the bog became cracked and parched, with only the pools remaining wet.

I decided to cut peat for the fires the first year of living at Caolas, but lacked a tool for the job. A peat cutter is like a deep, straight spade with a right angle and a foot press. After asking around the area, I was offered the loan of one from John, a man in the village.

"Of course, you know that peat cutting is man's work," he informed me lugubriously, as he slowly tamped and lit his pipe. "Aye, man's work. Hard work. Aye. The women always brought the peats home, but the men always did the cutting."

It was obvious that this masculine job was thought to be far beyond my female capabilities. Undeterred, on the next dry opportunity I made my way over to the bog with a variety of spades, forks and the peat iron. Having decided which looked the most likely of the long disused workings, the top of the peat had to be exposed again. This meant removing the tangled heather and wiry grass with tough long roots. It was a bit like chopping into a Brillo pad. John's words echoed in my head as I fought to remove the tough vegetation.

The sun shone with that bright clarity of spring, the hillsides still wearing their bleached mantle of dead molinia grass and the east wind plucking strands of dead grass and tossing them into small whirlwinds that whistled and spun as they went tearing across the moor. The inner loch was rough, with waves cresting up to the narrows and a turbulence caused by the wind driven waves meeting an incoming tide.

With an area eventually cleared of top growth, I was ready to start on the peat. The hag was deep and had a vertical face of about three feet disappearing into the black, oozing morass of undetermined depth, as I found to my cost when trying a shortcut to pick up my iron from the other side of my workings. One leg sank to above the knee and I grabbed at the wiry heather on the bank to save me from sinking further. The wind had eased and it was growing quite hot, so off came my chocolate brown sodden jeans, which I laid on the bank to dry, then I tipped the excess water from my boot and carried on.

For a start, the peat was still full of roots and not easy to dig. The iron was quite rusty, but as I continued the blade became polished and the peat became easier to dig the further down I went. It was like digging out slabs of solid chocolate cake, the knack being to flick each piece up onto the bank before it dropped off the tool into the bog. Many times I had to climb down the bank and retrieve a half sunk block.

The day grew hotter and I became grubby and sweaty. The muddy t-shirt came off and joined the trousers on the bank to dry. It was a good job there was nobody around for miles. What a sight I was; covered in goo, digging away in bra, pants and wellies. I must have looked like a mud wrestler.

A Golden Eagle soared high above me and I stopped to watch its effortless flight. I could just see where the up current was riffling its wing tips.

"Hi eagle. Have you ever seen anything like this below you before?" I called.

The pile of peat on the dry bank was growing larger and I stopped digging to place three slabs at a time in little mini-ature "Stonehenges" to dry. The day was moving on and the sun was now shining fiercely onto my shoulders. The first bumble bees of the year droned noisily past and swarms of tiny insects hovered above the boggy water.

My rapt concentration was completely on the task in hand, digging and flinging, digging and retrieving, stacking and spreading out the wet blocks. Then I heard a sound; the toot of a boat's horn followed by two more toots. Now the tide was out and the higher ground between the hag and the shore effectively hid me from any small prawn boat passing through the narrows. This was obviously not a small boat. I straightened up and turned 'round to see a well known large charter boat of 70 foot or so long, its deck full of sight-seers slowly and quietly slipping through the narrows. The glint of sunlight on binoculars confirmed my fears that I had been spotted. Too late to grab my wet muddy clothes, I must have looked quite a sight in my undies and wellies. I wonder how many holiday snaps must have shown a bizarre figure covered in mud, miles from anywhere, brandishing a weird long handled spade.

Some months later in port I bumped into the owner and skipper of that boat and he reminded me of that day.

"Och aye," he said, grinning roguishly. "It was the high-light of the trip up the loch. I throttled back on the engines and just cruised into the narrows. Your face was a picture through my binoculars and not only your face." He emitted a loud guffaw of laughter.

During the next two weeks or so the peats dried well. I turned them regularly and then built them into small stacks ready for bringing home. The only way of moving them was in an old rucksack, the ground being too broken for a wheelbarrow. In the old days, when the peat was cut every year at Caolas, it would be the women who carried it home in large wicker baskets on their backs, the weight bearing on a band across the forehead. I loaded my rucksack full of the dried lumps of peat and set out across the moor. It would take a long time to carry all the peat home. I changed my transportation system to a large black dustbin bag in the hopes of getting more in, but the spiky blocks tore holes in the bags and each one would only last a couple of trips. It was hard, back breaking work stumbling across the broken ground. Women's work; huh!

Several days later, the wood store was nearly filled with dry and crumbling blocks, just ready for winter fires. What a lovely warmth and smell they gave off as we sat and toasted our toes in front of the heat, as the peats gently burned in the large grate the following winter.

Chapter Ten

Burrs in Their Tails

It had seemed a good idea at the time. I remember "the time" had been way into a roistering good ceilidh at a friend's house in the village. The inevitable moment arrived when we knew we were not going six dark miles home by boat that night. We were quite mellow and receptive to new ideas.

"They are a wee bit wild," Murdo admitted, as he downed another gulp of whisky, "but a bit of handling will sort them out," he grinned mischievously at us.

"They," in question, were two weaned Highland filly foals, straight off the hill.

"Well," I contemplated, before giving an answer. In the past I had broken in a couple of large thoroughbred types of horses, so Highland ponies should be straightforward. The price was negotiated over another dram and with the customary slap of the hand, the deal was completed.

It was a week or so later when the large local landing craft turned in through the narrows into the bay below our remote farmhouse. At first sight the flat deck looked completely empty, but as the craft scrunched gently onto the stony beach and the ramp lowered, we could see two shaggy little foals tied very securely by their heads to the side rails. The deck was constructed of slippery steel plate and both of them stood splay-legged to keep their balance. The voyage from the village had obviously been their first lesson in restraint and they were wild eyed as we approached.

"Hold on tight!" shouted Murdo as Johnnie, Pete and I gripped a rope. With a clatter of tiny black hooves, the first one careered down the ramp, the four of us unceremoniously dragged behind.

"Don't let the bugger go," grunted Murdo, as we tried to aim this hairy little creature up to the yard and into the stable. Sometime later and after much tugging and swearing, both of these wild, intractable ponies were stabled. Murdo had been spot on; they would need a bit of handling. Both were mid brown with black stubby manes, a black dorsal line down the middle of their backs and tangled black tails full of burrs.

Endless patience over the following weeks saw me leading them 'round their large stable. Elsa, the larger of the two, became quiet and gentle, but Isla was much more highly strung and, if startled, was likely to kick out very accurately with her hind hooves.

We had no fenced fields into which they could be moved, since the farmyard just opened out into a meadow full of wild flowers and onward to the surrounding mountains.

For their first foray out of the stable, we barricaded up the two entrances to the yard with an assortment of wooden pallets all tied together with baler twine. For several weeks this meant that any visitor to the house had to clamber over this swaying fortification just to get to our door. The ponies enjoyed this area of space and nibbled the cobbled yard clean of grass. They would come to the back door and gently pick slices of apple and carrot from our open palms.

The spring grass started sprouting spikes of green out in the meadow and it was time to let our young charges have their freedom. We were well aware that, once out of the yard, our babies could disappear for ever into the vastness of the huge area of wilderness behind. They snorted suspiciously as we dragged the pallets away, then hesitantly they stepped delicately over the indentation left in the grass. Suddenly, as if they had both been jagged with adrenalin, they kicked up their heels, farted copiously and skidded off across the stone cobbles and away across the meadow. They didn't stop. The sound of thudding hooves on the grass faded as their shaggy forms disappeared down the shoreline and over the craggy rise into the next bay.

"Oh well, that is that," sighed Pete, shrugging his shoulders in a gesture of resignation.

There was hardly a sound left, only the wind sighing in the old sycamore tree and the gurgling of the ebbing tide surging past the boat at moorings. We went about our daily tasks, sometimes momentarily peering down the meadow for any sight of the ponies. Not a creature stirred, not even any deer down to nibble the fresh green shoots.

I had left two buckets of horse food in the yard just in case they came back. Much later, as I was cooking supper, a thundering noise permeated the kitchen. It sounded like a cavalry charge. I opened the door to find the two of them back and stuffing their faces into the buckets. Their tails were full of dead bracken and brambles, their eyes shining. What a day of freedom they must have had; they were in heaven.

This became a regular routine and as spring progressed, they would sometimes spend several days away, only thundering back for titbits. They metamorphosed from skinny little beasts into shining, dappled, small ponies.

We were working hard on rebuilding the cottage and it was time to fit the new windows. For many years the two front windows had looked like vacant eye sockets staring forlornly across the loch. Now they looked complete again, finished with smooth soft putty around the frames. It was a job well done and we retired that night satisfied with progress.

The next morning, however, showed a terrible transformation. All the putty had disappeared from both windows. Luckily, the glass was still intact, but horribly smeared. There were teeth marks along the edges of the wooden frames. The obvious culprits stood not far away, still licking the residue of putty from their lips. Blessed ponies. Realisation hit us immediately. Horses love the taste of linseed and putty is manufactured using linseed. We had not thought to barricade the windows; the ponies were away and we had not seen them in days. They must have stolen back after dark and nibbled and licked all night. The frames were as clean as if someone had prised every bit of putty out with a toothpick. Back to work to clean the glass and replace all the putty, but how to stop the ponies?

I then had an inspiration. If I concocted a mixture of something utterly repulsive and painted it onto the new putty, it would taste so repugnant that they would not come near. I rummaged in the pantry and found potential horse deterring substances. There was curry and chilli powder, garlic, paprika pepper and an ancient bottle of syrup of figs that must have sat on the shelf since the last people had lived there. All stirred together into a sticky paste, this fiendish alchemy sent eye watering fumes into my face. As Pete finished smoothing each section, I followed behind with a small brush liberally laying on huge quantities of this mephitic, yellow goo. The ponies watched the whole procedure from a discreet distance as we were enfolded in the powerful aroma. The whole place smelt like an Indian restaurant as we walked back to the farmhouse.

We were quite confident that no pony would venture near a smell like that. Of course, we were proved wrong in the morning. Not only had the jalap been to their liking and every morsel of putty removed, but to add to this devastation all the glass was smeared bright yellow; the sort of yellow often seen in old church stained windows, but not as artistic. The yellow muzzles gave the game away. There were yellow streaks down their necks, over faces, down the wall, even on the surrounding grass. It took a lot of scrubbing to clean those windows.

An electric fence dug deep out of the back of the barn and one of the more obscure items that we had brought with us, was the only answer and set up all around the cottage, it kept the ponies away for several weeks until the new putty had dried.

The ponies grew into sturdy mounts and I spent a lot of time, when they deemed it appropriate, to stay at home getting them used to saddles and bridles. This I was able to accomplish quietly in the stable. They still lived out their life of freedom, sometimes away for several days before erupting in a flurry of hooves at the back door of the house and expecting food morsels. Their tousled manes and tails would be full of twigs and burrs; goodness knows where they went.

We were to keep them for a further two years while they grew and matured, before we sold them on to work for their living as "deer ponies".

Two very different ponies were to clatter up the ramp of the landing craft on that last day. Handsome, well grown, glossy coated Highland ponies, their manes and tails brushed out for the occasion.

I did wonder, however, as the boat disappeared from view, how they would accept the restrictions of living in a field in the village with boundaries, with no more forays into their secret wilderness.

Chapter Eleven

Unexpected Visitors

As it was not possible to just pop down to a shop for a loaf of bread, I made our own. We only had bought bread for the day or so after going into the fishing port. Usually, I made bread every two days using flour from a sack kept in a dustbin in the kitchen. I would mix and knead the dough first thing in the morning and leave it in a large bowl covered with a tea towel on the kitchen table. The Rayburn was always alight, even in the summer, as it provided our hot water as well as cooking and heat, so the kitchen was always warm. The dough would be left to rise all day whilst we carried on with the building works at the cottage, or any other jobs that we were doing. I would come back indoors at about 3.30pm and find the dough had risen right up to the top of the bowl.

Sometimes I would make it into loaves, but we became partial to smaller baps and that was what I had made one particular afternoon. After another half an hour or so of proving, the buns were ready for baking. I had already stoked up the Rayburn and the temperature was just right to bake them. In they went and I washed up the doughy bowl and stood at the sink looking out of the window.

I often stood and watched the narrows with the tide racing and tumbling in and out, or dead calm at slack water. It had followed this cycle for millennia with the unfathomable power of millions of gallons of water moving continuously one way or the other. I found it fascinating and awesome to watch. How hard the rocks must be in the narrows to withstand this daily pounding. It was racing past and the boat at moorings tugged at the chain, even though she was not in the worst of the maelstrom.

After a while, the delicious smell of baking bread emanated from the Rayburn, taking my thoughts away from the power of nature and I lifted the golden brown baps out of the oven and onto the table. They smelt wonderful. Almost as though he had received a signal, the back door opened and Pete walked in.

"Just let them cool a bit," I warned as he fetched the butter dish out of the pantry.

We had fetched a week's worth of mail earlier that day and now seemed to be a good time to sit and open it all. The bread sat on the table wafting us with an almost irresistible aroma.

About half way through opening the mail, there was suddenly a distinct tap at the back door. It wasn't the sort of noise that the ponies would make on the doorstep if they were at home; it was a regular "rat-a-tat-tat". Barney barked and we looked at each other. Nobody had ever just arrived at the door while we had been living there. Everyone who came to visit came by boat, which we could always hear approaching. Miles of pathless lochside precluded most walkers from venturing our way and in all the time I lived at Caolas, only half a dozen hikers at different times were ever seen passing the house. The tapping commenced again, this time louder and more insistent and the dog gave another bark.

"We'd better answer it," Pete said, as I tentatively got to my feet.

On opening the door, I was greeted by a sorry sight. There was a young man and woman, both almost on the point of collapse, the man holding the woman's arm. They had huge rucksacks on their backs weighing them down to a stoop.

"Oh, do come in." I opened the door wider and extended my arm to indicate the kitchen. They offloaded their heavy bags on the doorstep and stepped inside.

"Have a seat." I gestured to spare chairs around the table. Barney was ecstatic that we had visitors, for he didn't see many people nowadays. They sank gratefully onto the seats and I think that the girl was near to tears.

"Where are you from and what are you doing here so late in the afternoon?" we ventured.

I made them a cup of tea and gradually the whole sorry story came out. It was their first ever walking holiday and they had left their car far inland at the road end some twenty odd miles away to the east. They had planned to walk up the long valley from their car and over the pass and down to the sea loch. There they expected to be picked up by a ferry the next day after camping overnight at the head of the loch. At that time the current ordnance survey map showed the dotted line of a ferry service calling right at the head of the loch. This service had been withdrawn some years previously and these people had not checked prior to setting out for times and availability.

The full saga poured out. They had been waiting at the head of the loch for four days for a boat that was never going to arrive. They had seen nobody else during that time in spite of there being a regularly visited bothy and an occupied cottage. Our neighbours at that cottage were away at that time. This couple had run out of food and had found the initial trek over the mountains so difficult that they dismissed the idea of walking back to their car. From the head of the loch one could just see the house at Caolas six miles away and they must have decided that this was the way to go. I could only imagine their trek up the loch side with heavy rucksacks and no food. It was steep and pathless all the way. Most of the way was through wild oak woods with fallen branches and tussocks to hinder their progress. It had taken them all day to walk to our house and they were clearly exhausted.

"Would you like a bun?" I offered, when they had finished their story.

Most of the buns disappeared like spring snow off a dyke. They were ravenously hungry. I made more tea and they looked a lot better than when they had first arrived. I would be bread making again the next day!

"Can you run us to town tonight in your boat?" they asked.

"Sorry, no," we answered, for it was not long 'til it was dark and a round trip would take over three hours. There was a spring tide racing and picking up the mooring at night, in the dark and with a spring tide, was really difficult and dangerous.

"You are welcome to stay here tonight," we suggested and they agreed. A bed in the second bedroom was made up and quite early in the evening they disappeared to sleep.

The following morning, the rest of the buns were finished off and they asked about the possibility of transporting them out. It was mail boat day and the vessel would be arriving at the village just before 3pm. It was not a day that it would come up the loch. We had a very busy building schedule to complete for our employer and an unexpected long run to port was really out of the question. We had found that we could walk from Caolas to the village in about four to five hours and suggested that if they walked out, then they could catch the afternoon boat in plenty of time. They were well fed and rested and readily agreed to this. They heaved their heavy packs onto their backs; goodness knows what was in them. We waved them goodbye as they left the yard and made our way to work in the cottage.

Confident that they would have made the ferry with no trouble at all, we didn't hear a word on the radio for a couple of days. It then transpired, through a conversation with a friend, that they had stumbled exhausted into the village over eight hours after leaving us and had missed the ferry. How had they taken so long? They were obviously over-loaded and inexperienced and should have not have made a first walking holiday into such a remote area, but who were we to judge? We then felt rather guilty that we hadn't taken the day off and run them to town.

Chapter Twelve

Cometh the Power

"Now if you need any equipment or a generator when you are up there in the wilds, contact me because I can get most things," Frank had said at our last visit to his house before we left to live in Scotland. Frank was big in export and shipping and had offices around the world. If anyone could source something it would be him. After all, some years before we had bartered half a butchered bullock for an ancient but very reliable little grey "Fergy" tractor, which we had used on our small-holding in England.

His current assignment before we left had been to supply condom making machines to Nigeria. Of course, in the interests of providing faultless equipment he had manufactured a test quantity of these at his depot, much to the amusement of his staff. I'm not sure who tested them!

It was nearly a year since we started rebuilding the cottage and with the roof finished, wiring for an electric supply was being laid inside. It was time to source a generator and we thought about Frank. We were short of any bullocks to barter, but he wrote a letter back saying he could get us a big generator just right for our needs. Apparently, he was in the process procuring a shipment of compressors for the Middle East and each one came with its own separate generator. It sounded ideal and we wrote back to secure one.

For the first eighteen months at Caolas while we lived in the old house, we had no electricity at all. Light was provided by paraffin Tilley lamps, which shed their soft glow to our rooms.

The gentle hissing and the warmth given off by the pressurised containers contrasted with the cold sleety gales often crashing against the thick outside walls.

There was always a certain discipline each morning to fill these lamps from the paraffin drum, which had been brought in by boat and stood in the byre. Every winter morning the lamps had to be filled for the night, but as the days became longer and spring progressed, we found that sometimes the lamps felt heavy and only needed filling every other day. It was a sure sign that the days were stretching out. The bathroom was always lit by candles placed all around the bath. It was quite romantic, except that on a windy night the tiny flames would gutter and sway, threatening to extinguish as the huge draughts blew through the gaps in the wood lining of the wall. I would lie deep in the hot water and not want to leap out into the cold and run to the fire in the sitting room to dry off.

We had no television and I don't think we missed it. Even when we moved to the cottage with electricity and bought a set, we couldn't get a signal due to the high hills all around. These were times before satellite dishes. It would become a video only machine. We did have a battery powered radio with a voracious appetite for new batteries. The signal was not always good, but many nights we sat by a roaring log fire in the soft light and listened to music. It was also our lifeline to news and, more importantly, the shipping forecast. There was no vacuum cleaner to clean the house, but a brush and dustpan was adequate as most of the floors were old wooden boards with scatter rugs on top, which could be shaken in the yard.

The only modern device I found I really missed was a spin drier to wring the wet washing. Washing clothes was not a problem, because with endless hot water from the Rayburn, I could fill the huge cast iron bath with steaming hot water, tip in a quantity of soap powder and all the dirty washing, let it soak for an hour or so to cool and then take off my trousers, climb into the bath and stomp up and down in the soapy water, rather like treading grapes to make wine. On a cold raw winter day, it was warming and quite therapeutic. The clean rinsed clothes wrung out by hand then took several days to drip dry, especially if it was wet and sometimes ended up on a line in the byre. We were still some months away from moving into the cottage with all the modern conveniences.

We took time off from the cottage work to build a sturdy wooden shed to accommodate the generator. It was built about eighty yards from the house in the hopes of dissipating the sound, especially as it was a rather large generator that was due to arrive. About an acre of ground around the new shed was enclosed by deer fencing and we planted a quantity of tree seedlings to grow and eventually hide the prominent shed in years to come and also act as a baffle for the sound.

The generator arrived on the estate landing craft some weeks later. It was a beast of a machine and rated at thirty seven KVA, enough to light a small village. We were only proposing power for two houses. The JCB groaned and dipped alarmingly with the weight as it carried the generator from the landing craft to the shed and with a lot of combined shoving on wooden beams, the machine was finally set in place on the concrete plinth.

"We will need an oil tanker moored in the narrows to keep this going," Pete muttered morosely as the last holding bolt was secured.

It was then that Pete, with sharp eyes, read a metal plate attached to the side. Apparently the generator was set for industrial use on a three phase supply and not suitable for domestic use. What were we to do? It would blow anything up if we used it for the cottage.

"Well the only answer is to get Bob in," suggested James on the radio. "He will be able to change it to single phase."

That suggestion started a long and frequent business relationship and friendship with "Bob the Generator." Bob came from Aberdeen and for some years had serviced and supplied generators to remote places up and down Western Scotland. He had the reputation of being a wizard with any generator problems.

We fetched him from port several weeks later and during the two days he spent with us, he worked tirelessly altering the generator. We were at last ready to roll and the big machine was finally struck up. What a noise! It was deafening near the shed and could be still heard loudly at the cottage.

The first power tools on the building site were struck up and the first lights switched on. There had never before been electricity at Caolas and the half finished cottage shone like a Christmas tree. The trade off was, of course, the noise. The beautiful silence was gone. No more sounds of oystercatchers piping on the beach, or the racing tide in the narrows, the wind in the long grass in the meadow, or sighing in the old tree. I was horrified and quite distraught. What were we doing to this pristine, peaceful place? Pete and Bob didn't seem bothered, because we had power at last to work the necessary tools to finish the building work. I just couldn't come to terms with the fact that all day while work progressed and in dark evenings this cacophony of noise would assault the place. I even walked around to otter bay and could still hear it echoing off the surrounding hills. I couldn't get it out of my mind that we were destroying the very peace that we had come there for. It was obscene. I would rather have gone on wringing the clothes out by hand than have this continuous noise, but I would just have to accept it. I think I have always been a bit of a Luddite about progress.

The building progressed well for the next couple of months. We took in extra hands to speed the work on and power saws and drills buzzed every day. The "genny" roared on continuously. Rooms were formed inside the cottage and open stairs of beautiful local seasoned wood were constructed. We planned to move from the old house to the cottage in the spring.

During this time, our many trips to port for supplies were also necessary to procure an endless succession of drums of diesel for the generator. It had an insatiable appetite and cost a small fortune to run. It soon became apparent that it was way too large for our needs. Bob was consulted and he agreed that a much smaller generator was adequate.

Luckily we found a buyer for the beast almost immediately and the landing craft was booked again. Bob arrived on the same day that the generator was due to leave and brought with him two small green Lister generators, the type we had come to see at all the local houses. One was a seven KVA, sufficient to run a washing machine and any power tools and the other, a four KVA, for when we only needed light. The beast was dispatched on the landing craft and Bob spent another busy couple of days installing the new machines. What a difference. There was no more of that ear-shattering roar, just the burbling of a small engine within the shed. It could still be heard at the cottage, but the decibels were greatly reduced. I was happy again. I would still have a washing machine in the cottage, but we wouldn't be compromising the peace of the place.

That winter saw us still in the old house filling Tilley lamps and having baths by candlelight again, but I did have a brand new washing machine set in the new kitchen of the cottage amongst all the paraphernalia of building, which made such a difference.

No more stomping in the bath to get warm on a winter's day.

Chapter Thirteen

Re-fitting the Boat

James ran a neat, efficient boatyard full of neat, efficient craft; at least until I sailed into his life.

"Oh gawd, it's her in that bloody floating wreck again," I could imagine him saying, as I tried to sidle unobtrusively into his bay. This was the time of the full facelift. I thought he was lucky to get the contract, but he thought otherwise. After all, he had moved up there for a peaceful life and the boat and I would be staying for several weeks.

Pete and I had managed with the boat for nearly a year since purchasing her and undertaking the adventurous journey up the west coast to Caolas, but it was soon clear that there was a lot wrong with her. The major fault was the engine, which would cut out at regular intervals and would not start again until the fuel line filter had been changed and the fuel system bled through to expel all the air. This generally happened in a rough sea in close proximity to sharp rocks or cliffs.

James was asked to do a survey and had come to the conclusion that the engine problem was caused by the fuel tank being level with the engine and so the fuel pump would be working constantly, particularly when the level of diesel fell. Half empty and in a rough sea, the fuel would slosh around and air bubbles would form in the old pipes and cause the engine to stop. Her gear box was also faulty and the decks too low, allowing water to flood into the engine situated under only the loose rubber mats.

The catalogue of inefficient parts went on and on and our very understanding employer decided to install a brand new 80Hp Ford marine engine and gear box, raise the fuel tank and re-deck her with proper engine hatches and along the way replace all the other faulty parts. She would end up like a new boat.

Up on the slip the next morning, we surveyed the wondrous scene. I followed behind as James moved about, writing scribbles on a notepad and tutting.

"It's not my fault." I heard myself saying lamely. "She arrived like this. This is all the paraphernalia of her life as a fishing boat."

I received a sideways glance. He was still tutting as he started ferreting around amongst the "deck accessories.".

"I know what you mean by 'junk rigged'," he grunted, as he heaved two heavy iron bars over the side to clang loudly on the slip below. They had been keeping the engine hatch, or what passed as an engine hatch, in place. For an hour or so it was not safe to come within twenty yards of the boat and the heap of detritus on the slip grew impressive.

"There's going to be no more of these Firestone fenders," he muttered, as four perished tyres and their tatty ropes sailed over the side. I now know where the saying, "Clear the decks" comes from. He had really got the bit between his teeth now as he stepped, or rather fell into the wheelhouse.

"What's this?" he spluttered, as he heaved out an upturned wooden fish box.

"That's my pedestal," I said. I was trying to be funny by then; all else was lost.

You see, the wheelhouse was built for persons between about 5 feet 9 inches and 6 feet 2 inches. This critical measurement meant that anyone shorter than 5' 9" couldn't see over the bow when underway and anyone over 6' 2" would have a permanent stoop. I fell somewhat below this criterion at around 5' and needed at least one upturned fish box to stand on to see ahead when we were doing eight knots. Over the side went the fish box. It would probably be used for rearing leek seedlings in Maria's vegetable garden next year. Assorted worn shackles and a tin of rusty magnetized screws went over the side. They had served no purpose other than to deflect the compass by about 30 degrees. The rout was complete. I wondered how he was going to get rid of all this junk. I could imagine him, weeks later, still carting this rubbish out into the sound in his boat and in an impetuous frenzy lobbing it all overboard like some mine laying operation.

Up came the old decks. There was nothing delicate about this, just a lot of grunting and crowbarring up. For the next few weeks I worked quietly at one end of the boat, stripping and repainting, whilst he fitted the shining new blue engine and gearbox, rebuilt the decks and constructed a new wheelhouse roof. There was, however, a small altercation between us one day. I'd just finished painting a gloss finish when he started grinding some glass fibre and the breeze carried the shards of fibre onto my wet paintwork.

Some weeks later the metamorphosis was complete. Like the ugly duckling the old boat emerged swanlike one day, gleaming. There was even a designer stand for short skippers. The white boot top was level and matched both sides, even if it had involved sticking on copious quantities of masking tape to form a straight line on a blustery day. The night arrived when she was finished and the tide was right for putting her back down the slip and into the water. Tide would be right at about 4am and the anti-fouling of the bottom of the boat should be accomplished within a few hours of refloating.

It had been a typical West Highland summer day, "dreich" and midgy. The paint brushes stayed in the boat shed. What followed though was pure farce.

There were visitors staying on holiday at the time and they were all willing to help if it stopped raining. James and Maria had endured me staying at their house for about a month and he wanted to "paint my bottom" and get me away. The drizzle continued and we all sat down to one of Maria's veritable feasts, washed down with inordinate amounts of Rioja. The mood was distinctly mellow as we dabbed our lips with napkins. Suddenly, the last rays of watery sunshine lit up the room.

"Let's go," echoed around the room.

"Anti-fouling on," announced "himself" as he raised the cheese knife in a defiant gesture.

There were six or seven of us brave souls who tramped out into a midge infested evening. The lucky ones got the paint rollers on long handles. I was unlucky and had to crawl under the bilge keels to paint the inaccessible bits. You will understand what that is like if you have a boat. A lot of banter and verbal abuse passed between the volunteers and the slip received quite a smattering of red paint. Nowadays people pay to go paint balling, but this was free entertainment. Several of us concentrated as hard as we could in our wine induced state to paint a straight red line against the white boot top, but we kept colliding.

It was almost dark when we finished. There was just time to get a couple of hours' restless sleep ahead of the rising tide. In the cold light of morning, the anti-fouling had a distinct wavy line where it joined the white paint. Only four of us turned out for the launch; our heads were distinctly muzzy. The tide rose so slowly and eventually I eased the floating boat off the trolley and into the rising water and headed quietly out of the bay. James and his wife waved me away as I rounded the point and headed for home. What a wonderful boat she had become and she gradually filled me with confidence every time I took her out. Nobody was now going to call her "The Collapso".

Chapter Fourteen

Sea Harvest

How could one live right beside a sea loch and not try a bit of fishing? The otters, often spied nearby and the motionless herons waiting to stab a passing fish, suggested a rich and varied life below in the depths. I was a complete novice about all fishing matters and so I quizzed local people to find what I needed and how to start.

My first "darra" for fishing mackerel was homemade out of a piece of floor boarding from the building site. It was notched at both ends, onto which I tied about 30′ of fishing line and wound it up. Then, from the chandlers in port, I bought a length of line with hooks spaced at intervals and with brightly dyed chicken feathers attached to these hooks. An old metal bolt made a weight to help it all sink and I was ready to try it out. I also made a simple rod out of a hazel branch with a length of line, a hook and a weight. A small piece of polystyrene, also from the building site, made a float.

Sometimes, on light summer evenings after a day's work on the cottage, if the tide was slack, it would be pleasant to push out the new rubber dinghy into the narrows, row one way and gently drift back, the polystyrene float bobbing behind.

The centre of the narrows was deep and dark, although shallow by comparison with the waters of the inner and middle loch, which had been ground out by glaciers in the last ice age. When the flowing glacier had come to the hard rock in the narrows it had stopped and deposited millions of tons of silt, rocks and pebbles, which formed the flat ground around Caolas.

I would mostly catch Pollack or "cuddies" as they were known. When cooked, they had the texture of cotton wool filled with needles. My limited culinary skills never made anything more palatable, so I lost interest in fishing for them.

The mackerel, however, were wonderful. They were especially delicious if cooked within an hour of catching and were well worth going farther out in the loch to catch. They were absent for most of the year, being somewhere out in the ocean, but they would start running into the sea lochs in early summer. Sometimes the shoals would be easy to spot as gulls would wheel screaming above, before diving onto the boiling surface to pounce on the tiny fish forced up to the surface to escape the feeding frenzy of the mackerel below.

We were out on the loch late one glorious evening in the big boat. The egg-yolk sun cast an orange glow onto the loch surface and cast long dark fingers of shadows into the gullies of surrounding hills. We were making for a headland about two miles down the loch as someone suggested it was a good place to try for fish. Suddenly, off to our left, we spied gulls diving in one area right in the middle of the loch. We turned and approached slowly, cut the engine and drifted towards the noisy melee. We had hardly dropped the darra over the sides of the boat and into the water before there was the tug of a hit and then another, the line jerking and vibrating with each fresh hit. The water was clear enough to see the silver flashes as the mackerel hurled themselves at the feathered hooks. The line, which was heavy with plunging fish of vibrant silver and blue black colours, was landed on the deck. There is an art to taking mackerel off a darra without the empty hooks tangling with each other and piercing slippery hands.

With the fish despatched and in a bucket, we cast again. We took another bucketful, which was all we really needed. We did not believe in taking more than we needed and it was too late to take a catch to sell at the village. We left the gulls, which had moved to another shoal and turned for home. In all the years since that first mackerel event, I have never forgotten the thrill of feeling the fish pounce with powerful thuds onto the line.

The sun had set and all was in quiet shadow as we gutted our catch back over the side of the boat into the dark waters. On our way home, we drew into the inlet where Donald lived. Our hollering brought him to the door of his house. He knew exactly what we were waving in an old plastic shopping bag as we pulled alongside the rocks and flung the bag of fish ashore. Shouts of "Thank you!" echoed across the dusky inlet as we turned and headed for home.

I acquired a monofilament salmon net. All these years later, I cannot recall how or where I purloined it. I only knew it was illegal to own or use one and this was the lure. It just had to be tried. The danger of being caught was so deliciously wicked, like creeping unseen into an orchard as a child to scrump apples; only worse.

I untangled and laid out my acquisition on the flat turf by the house to see how big it was. This was carried out almost furtively in case anyone could see what I was doing, which was ridiculous because anyone coming by boat would be heard long before they arrived and the chances of hikers coming along the pathless loch side were very slim.

Wild salmon spend some years maturing in the far oceans before coming back to the very river where they were spawned to mate and lay eggs before dying, so that the whole life process begins again. They sense or smell the fresh water as they approach land and this is heightened if heavy rain has swollen the peaty water tumbling into the sea.

It was such a morning, ideal to try out the net. Heavy rain in the night had swept away at dawn to a shimmering clearness where every blade of grass and leaf was adorned with droplets. It was cold and fresh as I pushed the rubber dinghy out and struck up the wee outboard engine. A cormorant flapped heavily away across the narrows and I disturbed a heron as I rounded the sand bar. I was off to the tiny horseshoe bay just down the loch, which has a large burn emptying over a gravelly beach into the sea, an ideal place I thought to try my luck. I travelled past the otter holt on the small island, where previously I had seen a family of otters, and around the headland. The tiny bay was still and almost perfectly enclosed by the rock bastions guarding its entrance. As I cut the engine, the only sound was the swollen burn tumbling its waters onto the shore. The inlet was in shadow and cool as I cast out the net across the narrow opening and clambered ashore each side to secure the ends to boulders. The mist was now lifting from the surrounding mountain tops, the last streaky clouds a distant memory of a wild wet night. The sky was cerulean blue as I turned for home, mission accomplished.

All that day as I worked, I wondered about the net, so it was with huge anticipation that I set out very early the next morning to gather my catch. The reality, however, was somewhat different to my fantasy. Something had been around the net, but as I hauled it on board it was hopelessly tangled with seaweed and very heavy, but yielding no salmon. Two seals surfaced not far away to investigate this intrusion. We were all after the same game, but they were much better at it than I was. They scrutinised me boldly with their large round eyes for a few minutes before turning their whiskery noses skywards and disappearing silently below.

I never did catch a salmon with that net, but I was not really bothered; it was just fun to try. However, I did once nearly get spotted as I was engrossed in my nefarious task of hauling in another catch of seaweed at a likely spot further up the loch. It was very early one morning and half the tangle of cleaned net was in the dinghy and I was working away clearing the forest of weed at water level, when I heard a boat engine. We had become much more attuned at Caolas to hearing strange noises, particularly man made, for most of the time the only sounds were natural. I knew most of the fishermen who fished the loch and at this time of high summer they would all be fishing further out to sea. It was only about 5.30am so maybe someone else was poaching. The thought made me smile to myself. I was in a dilemma as the sound was rapidly getting closer and soon a boat would appear 'round the headland. I had no time to clean off the other half of the net; I just hauled it weed and all into the bottom of the boat where I tried to cover the whole slippery mass with my waterproof coat.

A well known boat came into sight just as I was innocently casting a line from my home made rod. He knew me and I knew him and I don't think he was fooled. We waved cheerfully at each other and he continued on his way.

I found four creels at different times of beachcombing on the long sandy beach at the front of Caolas. They had all been washed up by storms and were slightly the worse for wear. A bit of straightening and some inventive weaving with fishing twine made them serviceable again.

Just through the narrows and on the opposite side of the loch was a rock face dropping sheer into the loch and I had been told that this was the sort of territory favoured by lobsters. There was no hauler on the boat to haul up all four creels together, so I would have to cast each one individually. I purchased enough rope to attach about fifty foot to each creel and a float. The pink floats had been found washed up on remote beaches up and down the loch during many trips.

One calm, fine day seemed a good time to try and catch a lobster, so I set out in the big boat with my fleet of four creels. The water was deep and clear, right up to the rock face, as I carefully nudged the boat forward. Hoping that there was enough rope to reach the bottom, I gingerly lowered each creel at about fifteen foot intervals. The ropes went slack as each one touched the rocky bed below and the pink floats bobbed on the surface.

Back home and using binoculars, I could just see the four floats against the dark loch and the cliff face. I had hoped to catch a lobster on my first try and was disappointed the next day when all I had caught were rather indignant spider crabs. This situation repeated itself for a week or so. I changed my bait from cuddy heads to mackerel heads and even sausages, but all I got were the hairy legged crabs. My atavistic attempts at procuring wild food for my family were not succeeding.

I was willing to give it one more try. It was not an ideal morning as a strengthening north westerly wind was causing a swell to run straight into my fishing area. I would not be able to move in too close for fear of the waves sweeping me against the rock face. Going as close as I dared, I leapt out of the wheelhouse and quickly dropped the first baited creel before diving back through the door to thrust the boat into reverse away from the black rock. The wind was tossing the branches of the birches high above and the waves were beginning to pound against the slimy rock as I cast the other three creels. Job completed, I backed quickly away from danger. I noticed that there were two other numbered floats not far away, belonging to a local man who certainly knew what he was doing. Maybe the next day would be my lucky day.

Looking through my binoculars from the house the following morning, I could not see my floats. In fact, all the floats had gone. There had been a high spring tide and the wind had changed to the south west. I feared that my creels may have been tumbled into deeper water, or blown into the narrows and lost. The tide was falling as I reached the spot where they had been cast and I leaned over the side to look down into the clear deep water. There was not a sight of them anywhere, only barnacle encrusted rocks and sea urchins.

Disconsolately, I turned for home and was heading back into the narrows when something caught my eye. Away off to my left and almost on the sandy shore of the bay were floating four small pink floats. How on earth had they got there against the current? As I headed for them, the water became considerably shallower and I could see the sandy bottom littered with star fish. With a draught of over four foot I had to be careful not to beach the boat, especially on a falling spring tide. It was easy to see the creels below and the long lengths of rope floating on the surface threatened to wind around the boat's propeller. They were lying in only about ten foot of water and as I hauled the first two in, the bait had gone, but I hadn't caught a thing. The third one was heavier and as I raised it towards the surface I could see something inside. As it broke surface there was a large, shiny lobster inside, its hard carapace a deep gun metal blue and black. It waved its snapping claws menacingly at me as I carefully lifted it out. I was astounded. It was not possible to catch a lobster at this spot; even I knew that.

A slow realisation dawned on me. The fisherman who owned the other fleet of creels had been to collect his catch and it was now obvious that I had unwittingly placed my creels on top of his creels, which is a totally unacceptable thing to do and would cause all sorts of problems in hauling out. It was made worse by the fact that I knew this fisherman from the number on his floats and he was a delightful man, well into his 70s, still fishing for his living. He could have so easily cut my creels loose in the deep water, but the only explanation that I could reason was that he popped a lobster into one of my creels, taken them over to the sandy bay and dropped them there as if to say, "Here is a lobster, but keep away from my creels or I won't be so benevolent next time."

I don't know to this day if that is what happened, but I was always careful after that experience not to shoot my creels anywhere near anyone else.

That evening meal was special as it was our first lobster and we ate like royalty.

Caolas cottage when we first arrived

Unloved and abandoned

89

Caolas farmhouse where we lived whilst rebuilding the cottage

The view east from near the house

The sycamore tree, farmhouse and mountains at the head of the loch

The Narrows at Caolas seen from the far shore

The landing craft arrives with a load of building materials

Work well underway at the cottage

The ponies Elsa and Isla

The Calypso after the refit

Looking west from Caolas

My father and I in the wheelhouse of the Calypso

The finished cttage

The cottage dining room

Near Magic Wood looking towards the head of the loch

Stag visiting the house for potato scraps

Barney

Caolas on my return in 2007

Chapter Fifteen

Grunters and Chooks

The sea gives life and the sea takes life and every generation of fishing families anywhere has sad stories of the loss of their men folk at sea. It is not surprising that superstitions have grown over the centuries surrounding boats and the men who make their living from them.

When we first decided to buy and transport in some weaned piglets and use them to plough and grub up the piece of ground that had been newly fenced for a vegetable garden, we hadn't reckoned on the reaction of our acquaintances in port. Some had recoiled in horror and I was quietly drawn aside and sternly informed that it was bad luck to mention pigs anywhere near a fishing boat.

"Whatever started that superstition?" I asked incredulously, but I was met with a dismissive shrug of shoulders.

"Nobody will take them up the loch for you," the bearer of information stated firmly through pursed lips.

I had wondered why, on mentioning my agricultural plans over coffee in the Fisherman's Mission the Friday before, that people had, well, sort of dispersed. We put our plans on hold for a time while I conducted a spot of research. Murdo seemed a good fund of local knowledge and I picked his brains one day in port. He looked serious and reiterated that it was considered bad luck to transport pigs on a fishing boat and something ominous would happen sooner or later. It was made clear that to call them "grunters" rather than pigs lessened the prophecy of doom. I also learnt from him that no one will go out from port on Friday

13th, especially in the morning. Mentioning swans or seeing them was also taboo; even a box of matches with a picture on it of a swan was prohibited. Seeing red headed girls and nuns would also keep any self-preserving skipper firmly in harbour. There was an obvious dearth of nuns in port, but there was a fair smattering of red headed lassies.

Murdo reluctantly agreed to run our grunters from port to Caolas, subject of course to none of the above phenomena happening on the morning. It all went off quite well and two small grunters arrived on the landing craft stowed in a strong pallet cage wedged between more building materials for the cottage. I decided not to ask how the loading went in port, for past experience had taught me that a firmly grasped weaner pig lets out the most ear piercing of screams. I wondered whether anyone had put out to go fishing that morning.

"Thank you for the p—grunters." I waved merrily to Murdo as he climbed back into the wheelhouse to back the craft away from the shore. I was still waving a little uncertainly a couple of minutes later as there was a lot of revving and wash, but he was not moving at all. He was out of the wheelhouse and peering over the side.

"I'm bloody stuck,' he shouted. "I knew something would happen bringing those bloody grunters."

A few weeks later and the pigs had settled well and were growing fast. After a bit of discreet research, which determined that there was no superstition about hens on board a fishing boat, we decided to purchase a few young pullets. It was always difficult bringing eggs from port as often they would arrive home cracked after being wedged with other shopping, gas cylinders, drums of fuel and building materials. It would also be good to see a few hens running about the meadow outside the house. I had never seen a pine marten there, but we knew there were foxes, so a strong house would need to be constructed. Nobody locally seemed to sell young chickens, but everyone we asked spoke of a Mr Mac who lived in a village on Skye.

"Och, just address a letter to him at that village and it will find him," we were told.

I compiled a short letter explaining that we had no telephone, but that we would like six strong pullets and because of where we lived they would have to be delivered to the pier at the fishing port on mail boat day. I posted the letter the next time the mail boat came up the loch and awaited a reply from the "chicken manny." Some days later, I was talking to Mary on the VHF radio and during the conversation she mentioned that our hens would be on the mail boat sometime the following week. The Highland grapevine was working again. Sometime the following week turned out to be Friday, as we heard on the radio, and we took the boat to the inlet to wait for the arrival of the mail boat.

As the bigger boat stopped, we drew alongside and exchanged greetings and some news; they were always interested in how the building work was coming on. A large cardboard box with holes skewered in the sides was passed down to us. There were clucking noises coming from inside and the frantic scrabbling of feet. I could just see a beady eye staring out at me. We got the hens back to the moorings, into the dinghy and ashore. The new wooden hen house sat just outside the garden awaiting their arrival. They were carefully placed inside and with rapid, nervous blinking of their eyes they explored their new home. I wondered how long it had been since anyone had hens at Caolas. They settled in well and we also acquired a cockerel called Cedric from the village, so the six brown hens could be seen contentedly scratching in the meadow with their attendant white rooster and we had lovely eggs.

There was, however, a rather disgusting habit that they suddenly adopted. It coincided with the arrival of a different bag of dog food from the normal one. The ingredients contained quite a significant amount of crushed grain. The dog was not impressed, but the chickens were. Hens are opportunists and it didn't take them long to find the odd, tasty dog turd lying in the meadow. It was full of undigested grain. Yes, you have guessed. In a flurry of feathers they fought with intensity over this booty. The dog would wander, as dogs do, over the field, sniffing and cocking his leg, with a retinue of hens in attendance. They had soon learned that this morsel suddenly and mysteriously appeared from the rear of this large furry animal. Barney would stop at his precisely chosen place and hunch up. A coven of hens would gather around him and if I wasn't quick enough to race down the field and scoop the poop, they would launch themselves into the steaming pile. This repellent behaviour carried on for some time and our passion for the beautiful golden yoked eggs diminished completely.

We had to do something. There was still half a bag of this inferior dog food left and two full trays of uneaten eggs. A different variety of dog food with no grain was ordered by radio and we fed the grainy stuff straight to the hens. Of course, they didn't enjoy it with the same exuberance as when it had been canine modified. The repellent habit was thwarted though and our appetite for eggs returned. Again, the hens returned to scratching worms and slugs in the meadow and straying down to the beach to pick tiny shrimps from under the sea weed. All was well again.

Chapter Sixteen

Caolas: A Love Affair?

Every time that I came back to Caolas, I felt a deep sense of homecoming. My ancestors are from Southern Ireland and England and as far as I know I have no historical links with the Scottish Highlands. In all the places that I have lived, a great part of me has always belonged in a place like this. Maybe it's because I have always been at one in wild, remote countryside, where my neighbours are deer, wild cats and eagles. Yet I knew my life at this enigmatic place would only be a fleeting moment in its existence.

My utter love for the place was also rocked at times when I lived there and on occasions I wished I was anywhere else. Usually these times were when the sea and weather were hurling their worst at me. We would be wet, cold and frightened and wondered what sort of mania had driven us to choose a life so full of dangers and uncertainties. After many a wild and scary passage up the loch, I'd turn the boat into the narrows and the sheltered bay in front of the old house and thankfully pick up the moorings with trembling hands. Then I would feel the greatest relief as the dinghy scrunched onto the pebbly beach, which was relatively calm compared to the wind that shrieked behind the spit of land.

Often several herons sheltered at the mouth of the burn, their heads hunched into their shoulders, looking comically like public school boys in a row, in grey suits and tails. We would tie the dinghy up high on the beach away from the water and make our sodden way up the well-worn path to the house where, on entering the kitchen, the warm heat from the Rayburn enveloped us and I would have an exuberant welcome from our dear old dog. All suddenly became normal again, the demons of the elements left behind as the solid, thick stone walls of the old house cocooned us from the storm outside. We had lived at Caolas just over a year and had seen it in all the moods of the weather.

It was not always stormy and early spring would weave its magic spell around us, with the awakening of nature in this huge landscape of sea, sky and mountains. Suddenly, there would be a proliferation of primroses along both banks of the burn, with delicate violets peeping from rock crevices. I'd lie on my back amongst the crackling dry grass of the previous year and watch the "V" formations of skeins of geese heading north to Spitsbergen, Greenland and who knows where. They always called to each other and keep altering positions at the head of the "V", their voices drifting down to me.

Spring would bring a new flush of grass; starting down in the meadow that ran right down to the beach, rich, green spears of growth pushed relentlessly up through the bleached old grass in a mantle of colour that spread progressively up the mountain sides.

Later, in early June, the meadow filled with purple and pink marsh orchids, like hundreds of strawberry ice lollies all standing to attention in the new greenery around. Overhead, skylarks called their sweet tune and meadow pipits flew upwards then plummeted, giving their lovely "see-er, see-er" sound.

I wandered in Coille Caolas, my magic wood. The oak buds had burst into leaves of different hues, firstly almost an autumnal shade of khaki, then the greenest of greens. There were no signs of human paths in this wood, which stretched about five miles down the lochside to a ruined settlement. I often followed deer tracks between the trees, or sat back against a mossy tree trunk full of damp earth smells and listened to the lovely descending songs of the warblers. I would almost feel absorbed by this place, so unique, as though by contact with the living things around me made me at one with them. It was a special feeling.

I once saw a wild cat in the bay between Caolas and the wood. Eye contact was brief before it turned and vanished quietly into the bracken. I never saw it again but I knew it lived around there. Thereafter, that bay was always referred to as "Wild Cat Bay".

A burn cascaded down from the corrie above into a deep pool near the shore of the bay and this pool made a wonderful Jacuzzi on a hot summer day. You could sit on a boulder under the falls with the cold water cascading down onto your head and shoulders. Nature had also provided a large, smooth, flat boulder nearby to lie on and dry after the shock of the cold massage. It was a good job hardly anyone came that way, as I would lie out naked and let the sun's rays warm me up, with the only audience possibly being just the wild cat nearby and the ravens swooping and croaking around the crags.

I made a list of all the wild flowers that grew around Caolas as they flowered during the summer. It was a sort of botanical calendar starting with the primroses and the tiny vivid blue milkworts, the fluffy sea of white cotton grass and the blousy pink orchids. Then, by mid July, the fly catching sundews would open and the bright, yellow spikes of bog asphodel would appear on the peat bog. Swathes of purple bell heather clothed the hillsides. Calluna Vulgaris, the common heather, adorned the hills in August, while the meadow would be full of nodding heads of blue scabious. A rare patch of Grass of Parnassus grew just up the hill behind the water tank for the house, showing its delicate white florets in early autumn. The rowan trees were already fully berried, suggesting an abundant feast for the flocks of redwings that suddenly arrived one day in October from Scandinavia and stripped each tree bare of berries.

By mid September, the grunts and roars of rutting stags permeated the night darkness. Days were growing noticeably shorter and the first of the equinox storms hurled themselves against the old house. The riotous flowering meadow would have seeded and the grass turned to russet brown before being laid flat by winter rain. I often stood near the very spot where I had laid in the spring and watched the geese flying south again. Could it be the same geese that I had seen six months earlier flying north? By mid October the countryside was a myriad of golden russet, yellows and red-browns in the slanting sunlight. The cacophony of stag passion echoed around the hills and then, by the end of October, it was all over. Their urges spent, the stags gathered together again in groups to come down and drink at the burn. They were ragged and exhausted.

Winter would soon be upon us again, the first storms of icy hail racing up the loch to slam against the walls of the old house. We'd awake one morning to an icing of new snow on the high tops and a chill in the air. My best photos were taken in the crispness and clarity of late autumn. On fine winter days I was often up amongst the high crags enjoying the pale sunlight, but on stormy days when outside work was completed, the tilley lamps would be lit early and a chair pulled close to a glowing peat fire.

Chapter Seventeen

December Dip

The tide was racing in full bore as we entered the narrows. Whirlpools like giant plug holes swirled the water crazily around and down and cresting overfalls of turbulent current surged and carried our boat at an amazing speed past the bay and house.

I had long since learnt that it was dangerous to try and pick up the mooring whilst being swept along by the tide. The only way to safely moor the boat was to sweep in a circle and power back against the current to the mooring buoy. That afternoon we were on high spring tides and millions of gallons of water were crashing their way into the inner loch. The current swept us perilously close to the skerry, which divided the waters as they careered up the narrows. I turned the boat across this maelstrom and pushed the Teleflex throttle fully forward. The engine roared as I headed into the powerful surge and immediately water crashed into the bows. We became stationary as the propeller fought to bite into the aerated water. The tide race was running at a good eight knots and the boat wouldn't go much faster than that. In the past I had seen boats turn back rather than fight the narrows at half tide and wait for calmer waters. The shore and the bank were just off to our starboard and the boat was still powered full out, but was stationary. Very slowly we started to make way as the propeller found purchase. The buoy was only fifty yards away and as I steered out of the main current, Pete went out of the wheelhouse to grab the small pickup buoy.

We were nearly home on a raw December afternoon after the long voyage from port. I pushed the boat, still on full power, up to the mooring and Pete grabbed the handle of the pink pickup.

To this day, I'm still not sure what happened next, but I can only think it was a sudden surge of current around the boat; a back eddy from the main race. Before Pete could haul the main mooring bridle onto the Samson post forward on the deck, the boat was swept sideways against the buoys and the chain rattled down the gunwales. I was scared to use any power with the chain now so near to the prop and hoped that the current would sweep us away from the mooring.

Pete had to drop the pickup. Such was the force of water thrusting the boat sideways, that he was in danger of being pulled overboard. The boat then rode right over the top of the mooring. There was a horrible clunk under the hull and we both peered over the side to see what had happened. The water creamed around the boat as the current tried to wrench us away, but we were stuck fast. The mooring chain ran under the boat and was snagged on either the rudder or the propeller.

We were moored by the stern. The raging current had driven us with such force onto the mooring that we couldn't free it. I cut the engine; we were not going anywhere.

How were we going to resolve this problem? The chain was down too far underwater to lever it out with the boat hook. We needed a diver to go down and free the snagged chain, but that was impossible. For a start, down in the bay we were out of radio signal with anyone. It was also about 3pm on a dark winter day and even if we had been able to raise anyone on the radio, by the time a diver had been brought from port, it would be dark. We obviously couldn't leave the boat precariously caught up by the stern, not with the vast tides we were having, in case

107

it became free and floated away. There was only one thing for it; one of us would have to try and dive down, see where the chain was snagged and attempt to free it, but we would have to wait another half an hour or so until the tide race lessened, as it would be too dangerous to swim in that current.

Pete couldn't swim, so he was obviously out of the equation. I had no wet suit and I knew I could only stay in a few minutes. As the tide lowered, we tried all ways with the boat hook to try and free the chain, but it was jammed solid just out of sight under the boat. The force of the tide had decreased and I stripped down to my underwear. Pete tied a length of rope around my waist, which he was going to hold in case I was swept away.

I climbed over the side and gingerly lowered myself into the freezing water, my breath suddenly uncontrollably expelled from my lungs. I gasped and panted and the skin on my scalp prickled with the cold. I had to get this over with quickly. I tried to steady my breathing, inhaled deeply and dived. It was to no avail. I bobbed back to the surface before I had even got near the chain, but I did have time to see that it was snagged between the rudder and the boat. Thank goodness it was not around the prop.

The current was still pulling me away as I dived again and tried to wrestle the chain free. It moved slightly, but I had to come up for air. I was becoming extremely cold and decided to have one more try. Pete held the rope and I lowered myself until just my nose and the top of my head was above water. I hung on to the stern of the boat and felt around underwater with my feet until I located the chain. It would only move sideways and not backwards and out. I would have to pass all the chain through the rudder under the stern, including the big pink buoy, which would be impossible as it was so buoyant.

Pete stabbed the buoy several times with the sharp boat hook and it burst. The whole weight of the mooring chain was held now by the thin rope and small buoy, which Pete secured to the boat. I started to manhandle, or rather foot handle the chain past the rudder, which seemed to take forever. The now deflated buoy was crammed through by my feet, aided by the boat hook, and at last we were able to extricate the rest of the rope from the small space between rudder and stern.

While I was achieving all of this, it did occur to me that I could be holding the whole weight of forty vertical feet of heavy chain with my feet, not a nice thought to contemplate if the small bridle rope broke. Thank goodness it was a success and the boat was free from the chain.

Pete pulled me back on board and found a whole bundle of dry orange winkle bags in a locker with which he rubbed me vigorously. I stripped off my wet underwear and clambered as quickly as I could into the rest of my clothes. The wind keened through my wet hair and I jumped around on the deck to get my circulation going. I think I must have been in the water no more than six minutes, but it felt a lot longer. Pete pulled the squashed buoy on board and pulled the boat round on the chain until he could moor it at the Samson post at the front. By this time, the tide had slowed completely and the boat lay still at moorings. We would have to shackle another big buoy onto the mooring the next day.

It was time to climb ashore and into a hot bath. It was only later that we both realised what a potentially dangerous episode it had been. I thanked my guardian angel.

Chapter Eighteen

Winter Reminiscences

I leant on the garden gate and watched the pigs rootling inside. How they had grown since the day they arrived on the landing craft. What had been rough grass and reeds inside the fenced area had been methodically converted by busy snouts into…well, mud. I stood watching them digging, their floppy ears flapping over their eyes. Pigs have a very calming presence and I was enjoying a short sojourn with them. They reminded me of a bunch of pigs we had reared many years ago when we lived in Hampshire. We had then recently become proud tenants of a very derelict and overgrown allotment. A fence was erected around the area and a pen of weaner pigs had been purchased from the local market.

The idea was the same back then as it was now; to clean up the ground ready for growing vegetables. At that time, I had worked part time in a very busy local pub. There were always plenty of waste slops from the beer pumps and these were all tipped into a plastic drum, which I would bring home for the pigs. Every feed time I would splosh liberal quantities of old ale into the corn meal and tip it into their trough. Feed times were always a frantic few moments until they all had their heads in the beery soup. When they had finished, they would wander a little unsteadily away and flop down against each other. Before too long there would be a porcine pyramid of gently heaving, grunting and burping flesh. This bucolic way of life continued all their short and happy lives. We often wondered if they suffered from hangovers, but nothing seemed to dampen their zest for the next meal. Not a lot of ground clearance was apparent, for they slept most of the time.

The memory made me smile. Two demanding snouts nuzzling the bucket of goodies I was holding bought me back to the present time. I took a few minutes while feeding these two left over fruit cake to reflect on what we had achieved that winter.

There was the continuing work on the cottage. The beautiful stairs constructed of local timber had been fitted and all of the rooms were in place. The drains had been laid and the big, onion-shaped plastic septic tank had been lowered by the JCB into a huge hole in the field. At this stage, a man from the council had to come along to test these drains. Sod's law, of course, dictated that the day we were to go down the loch and fetch him from port, there was a gale warning. I remember that he was waiting at the pier looking somewhat apprehensive as huge waves thundered against the harbour walls.

"It will not be too bad when we get round the point," I assured him, as we cast off from the steps. Poor man. He was subjected to several hundred yards of the most horrible huge sideways on sea as we left the calm of the harbour and rounded the point.

It did get better and a lot later and a little shaken we helped him off the boat and into the dinghy for the last stretch to the shore. We took him into the house and gave him a hot coffee and a very large dram, at which point he started speaking again. He hadn't uttered more than the odd word on the journey up the loch. He turned out to be an extremely nice man, who just didn't like boat journeys. His work took him all over the Highlands and sometimes boat trips were inevitable. He was to come several more times before the cottage was completely finished and, luckily, subsequent trips from town were relatively calm. He still got his dram though.

Christmas was fast approaching and our daughter Mandy was coming home for a visit from university. She had contacted us by letter and asked if she could bring a friend with her. He was a fellow student and of course he was welcome. We fetched in the last of the trimmings and food. The gas fridge was burgeoning with delicacies.

Mandy and her friend had decided to walk in over the hills from the railway station some ten miles away. There was a good footpath that would bring them to the opposite side of the narrows. I had just finished putting a mini glacier of icing peaks on the cake when I noticed two figures making their way along the shore. They had made good time and it was a still quiet day. The tide was out and the water in the narrows stationary as I pushed the dinghy out into the bay to fetch them. It was good to see Mandy again for we hadn't seen her since the summer. The new boyfriend was quiet and I think a bit overawed at the remoteness of our home. We all sat and drank wine in the warm kitchen while I cooked up supper and they told me about the complexities of life at university.

Christmas was great fun and the house came alive with shrieks of laughter. We fed our guests copious amounts of local lobster, crab, salmon, langoustines, venison and clams.

"Oh no, not more lobster," cried Mandy one day as we sat down to another veritable feast. "I shall be glad to get back to my flat for beans on toast."

The boyfriend must have thought that we lived this Sybaritic life style all the time.

They left by mail boat just before a big storm was due in the early new year and the house seemed strangely quiet for some time.

One day towards the end of that winter while Pete was busy in the cottage, I trudged across the peat bog and up to the water tank to clear the dead grass that I knew would have collected around the exit pipe. It precluded the need to have to attempt it one dark night when the water had already stopped; usually this would be just as you were about to have a bath. As I struck up the steep hillside I saw a pathetic sight ahead of me. Just below the tank by the burn lay a newly dead stag, his head hanging downhill and his legs splayed out behind him where he had fallen. Thank goodness, I thought as I passed him, that he hadn't died above the water tank and would therefore have contaminated our water supply.

The winter had been particularly wet and cold; the days of freezing sleet and rain had sapped the strength of all the wild deer. Many were to succumb and over the following weeks, I was to find several more dead animals in the vicinity.

Suddenly, out of the corner of my eye, I saw a movement. I froze; my eyes jerked back to his immobile body. I stood a minute and there it was again, the barest flicker of his ear and the almost imperceptive movement of his eyelids. I crouched quietly at his side and spoke to him. His eyelids flickered open and deep almond coloured eyes looked up at me. There was no fear there, for he was too weak.

I could do little for him except try and make him more comfortable, by moving him from his dreadful position hanging headfirst down the ravine. In spite of all the warnings I knew about not approaching an injured stag, I couldn't bring myself to just leave him. I grabbed his full set of antlers like they were bicycle handles and heaved with all my strength to try and move him round. Momentarily, he tried to struggle to his feet and I realised what a dangerous situation I was in. He could quite possibly gore me with those sharp points. I had moved him a little and by pulling down on his back legs I eventually started to get him more level. The hillside was so steep that he threatened to tumble down on top of me and he weighed something like thirteen stone, even in his emaciated state. He was an old stag past his prime who had survived many brutal winters, but this one looked like his last. I tucked his legs under him and stroked his neck. He watched me, but there was no resistance now. I like to think that he realised I was trying to help him and had made his position more comfortable, but maybe I was anthropomorphising.

I climbed the last few yards to the tank and cleared the debris around the water pipe, all the time talking to the poor stag in a soft voice. He was sat up, his ears twitching back and forward at the sound of my voice, but he made no effort to move. "Poor lad; he will be dead by the morning," I thought, as I left him quietly lying on the hillside. At least I hoped I had made his last few hours more bearable.

It was over a week later that I went up to the same spot, just expecting to see a corpse, but there was nothing. If he had died and a fox had ravaged his body, there would be tufts of hair, bones and antlers remaining. I smiled to myself, for maybe my efforts had helped and he had recovered.

Chapter Nineteen

Builder's Mate

It was a hive of activity at the nearly finished cottage. We had both been working hard for nearly eighteen months. I had been builder's mate, serving my apprenticeship. I had become a dab hand at mixing cement for walls and floors, helping to fix on hundreds of roof slates and forming wooden stud walls. My latest project had been to nail on what seemed like the harvest of a small pine forest, in strips of wood, to the formed walls. I was allocated the job of pointing the end stone walls, which were to be the exposed chimneys in the cottage. I was supposed to do the job using a small pointing trowel. Well, what a mess I made. In the end, I opted for pink rubber gloves and crammed the cement between the stones. Wire brushed the following day, it looked really good. Meanwhile, Pete did the complicated things like electric wiring and plumbing.

That particular day, he was taping and finishing the plaster board walls. I watched mesmerised as with fluent sweeps of his arm he plastered from floor to ceiling in one effortless movement. Each blob of plaster on his float creamed out neatly, sticking the narrow tape to the wall.

"That looks easy. Can I do that to help you?" I had the temerity to chirp. I knew that he wanted to finish the plumbing.

"Sure; just do it like I did," he grinned, passing me the board and disappearing back to the intricacies of the internals of a toilet cistern.

This is easy, I thought, as I cut a length of tape and scooped plaster onto my board. I was lost in concentration, my tongue between my teeth. Sweeping my float upwards, I made a first pass. Simple. Then taking the cut tape, which was curled up like a Christmas decoration, I swept the plaster float up the wall. It should have neatly stuck the tape in a straight line up the wall. The reality was somewhat different. The tape buckled in small concertinas, rather like pulled curtain rufflette under the float, and then fell off. I tried with a new tape with slightly more success, but then perversely that fell off and all the plaster with it. It was harder than it looked. Why was he so expert at so many things? I sulked churlishly as I scooped the amorphous mess off the new floor boards.

Admitting defeat, I watched him as, with an inscrutable face and just the hint of a smile playing round the corners of his mouth, he repaired my attempts, before I slunk off to hammer a few more timbers on the wall.

The council man made his last journey out to see us and to pass the cottage fit for habitation. The journey to completion had not been without its moments; for instance, when someone forgot to order a vital gasket for the back of the loo, we both blamed each other, but I pointed out that my department wasn't plumbing. "He" was not impressed by my excuse. It would involve at least another week of trotting to the old house for ablutions and more radio calls. A Heath Robinson seal was fabricated out of a piece of an old inner tube held in place tightly with string. It worked wonderfully once, but the second time, the pipe flew off the back and the inventor of this bodge received a wet surprise down his front when he flushed.

The frustrations of running out of skirting board in the last room and the angst of non-arrivals of the merchant's lorry, especially after a long boat trip into port, made us both a wee bit ratty.

At last it was finished and we were ready to move in. It looked beautiful. We were so proud of what we had achieved and we knew our employer would be impressed when he next came.

We had spent the previous eighteen months living in the old house without power and it was going to be such a revelation to have electricity at the flick of a switch. There had been a complicated system of relays fitted by the wizard generator man so that the first electrical switch would strike up the generator in the shed. After about a minute, when the generator had settled to a rhythm, another relay would send a signal to switch on the freezer. The last switch off in the cottage at night would cause the generator to shut down again.

A boatful of our wonderful friends from the village and beyond turned up one brisk April day to help us move the hundred yards or so from the old house to the cottage. The tractor and trailer were backed up to the door and our belongings were on the move again. Many shaky loads later and a lot of hilarity saw us finished.

The helpers left and we were alone at last, surrounded by boxes in our lovely cottage. It was the completion of phase one of the massive building project at Caolas and we experienced a huge sense of achievement.

As if to welcome us, the sun slipped down gradually behind the mountains and the last slanting rays brilliantly lit the kitchen as we ate a very welcome supper.

Chapter Twenty

Jungle Drums

All the vegetable seeds had arrived with the mail and as I checked each packet I envisaged a bumper crop in our new garden, well churned up and manured by the late pigs. We were salting one of the pigs for bacon and the other one was in our freezer. They had lived a short, but happy life with a shelter full of deep straw for sleeping in and the freedom to root and wallow in a rough pasture by day. Their dispatch had been humane and quick and the salting pig lay in a sweet cure on a stone slab in one of the byres attached to the old house.

We carted seaweed up from the beach to add more goodness to the soil and I dug large beds in the deep ground. This deep soil was entirely due to the millions of tons of soil and silt dropped at the end of the last ice age, when the glacier had retreated from the hard rock of the narrows.

April arrived and it was time to think about planting out seeds; my first rows were of peas and broad beans. Pete had made me a mini greenhouse that stood up by the south west wall of the cottage and in there I started lettuce and brassicas in trays. The daylight was extending well and after a very wet ending to the winter, we had day after day of keen, dry, cold easterly winds searing down the loch and drying up the ground. It was time to cut peat again; goodness, a year had passed!

Our employer and his wife came over from Belgium for a stay and his face beamed as he walked into the neat cottage.

They had not seen the build completed, as their last visit had been the previous autumn. We took them to the generator wood where the saplings were just burgeoning into leaf and to the garden where the first peas were arching out of the soil. The smiles never left their faces for their entire visit.

As we ran them in the boat back up to the village that evening, they discussed the next phase of the building project, which was the renovation and extension of the old house. When completed, they would use it as their accommodation when they stayed at Caolas. They planned to extend the living accommodation into the range of byres that were connected to the house and formed the square courtyard.

In the past, before coming to Scotland, I had completed working drawings for house extensions and I had now been asked to design and draw the plans for the old house. I was flattered, honoured and a little scared, for this was a massive project. My specification was to provide a large living room and more bedrooms and bathrooms, all fitting into the original shell of house and farm buildings. Windows would have to be knocked through the thick stone walls. On the journey back home from the village, my head buzzed with ideas. What a superb challenge. I hoped I was experienced enough.

The VHF radio in the kitchen and the one on the boat were still our only form of communication with the outside world. Most days I would radio the village to catch up on any news that had come though and sometimes there were messages for us. Usually though, it would be snippets of gossip; nothing too complicated.

Very occasionally there would be serious news. I called up one day as usual expecting to hear a cheery greeting at the other end. A strained, hushed voice answered my call. I knew immediately something was very wrong. I listened in horror as a tale of tragedy came over the air. A local fisherman had drowned under his boat. He had bought the Penelope from us. He was found tangled in the ropes of his fishing creels. In such a tiny community, everyone is well known to each other. We knew him well. He had been a lovely character with a young family. It was a sad time and everyone went to his funeral in the village. It brought home the dangers of operating a boat on one's own, for it was surmised that as he was casting empty creels back into the sea, a rope snagged his leg and the weight in the water of the rest of the creels dragged him down.

Thankfully, most of the radio conversations were much happier. I remember one well, which prompted the phrase "Jungle drums". We had not ventured for some time to the bigger town over fifty miles away. This was always a long day out, beginning with the time-consuming boat trip to port, followed by the road journey for much of the way, then by narrow single track road. A day in town called for military planning, as the shopping list would be extensive, with anything from building materials to dog food. It was the latter we were running rather desperately short of at that time.

It was possible by radio to get someone to phone an order in to the animal food supplier and a sack would be dispatched on the train to be uplifted from the station on the next trip to the fishing port. I had this in mind when I heard our neighbour's powerful boat throbbing down the inner loch towards Caolas. Our radio in the kitchen was on and I gave him a call up on the working channel that I knew he used. There was no reply. I tried again, but still the set remained quiet. I called call him on Channel 16, which was for call up as well as emergency. There was no reply again and the fast craft swished through the narrows and was gone from sight. He obviously didn't have his radio on, which was annoying. The radio, still on 16, crackled and a strange voice came on.

"Having a problem?" enquired a staccato voice.

"Go to 9," I requested, for I expected this was a fisherman and they mostly worked on channel 9. It was imperative to clear off the emergency channel as quickly as possible.

"Who is it?" I queried, after giving my own call.

The caller turned out to be a fisherman we knew well. He informed me he was fishing way out to sea in the sound. We chatted for a while before I came to the point of my call. I explained about our dearth of dog food and asked whether he possibly help that night when he got home by phoning on our behalf.

"I can do better than that," he informed me. I was sure he was laughing by now. "I will call up my missus on the CB radio and our next-door neighbour is off to town today. I'll get my missus to go 'round and ask her before she leaves. She will pick up a sack of dog food and you can get it from her house the next time you are in port."

All this was to be arranged over miles of sea. It was the ideal solution and I left him to start the arrangement. We had just enough food for Barney to last until a food trip on Friday.

Fairly early the next morning I could hear an approaching boat. The tide was out and I couldn't see who it was until they swung into the narrows. The weather was calm and most of the regular boats were fishing well out to sea, so who was coming up the loch? I could now see the boat of a well known fisherman who never came up the loch as far as Caolas. I wondered what he wanted and went to our radio.

"Hi there," a cheery voice greeted me. "I have a bag of dog food on board for you."

Well how was that for a quick service? And all down to the local "grapevine". He had made a special journey all the way up the loch to deliver it. Such was the kindness often shown by local people. I pushed out in the dinghy and rowed to his boat as he waited in the narrows. Just before I had left the cottage, I grabbed a dozen of our lovely free range eggs on a tray: small payment for all his time and diesel. We exchanged the sack for eggs and he pushed a further plastic bag into my hands. Imagine my pleasant surprise when I saw it contained a quantity of large, live prawns. Supper would be good that night.

Chapter Twenty-One

Canoeing with Porpoises

We were up at the village to make a phone call one bright late spring day, having come up from Caolas in the Calypso. The sky was a clear cobalt blue and the hills behind the village were brilliant green in their flush of new growth. The sun was warm on our shoulders as we tied up the boat at the pier steps. These were heaven sent days that helped one forget about the short dark stormy days of winter.

With the long distance phone call to Belgium attended to, the day was still stretched out ahead. We were having a well earned rest from building work.

"I'm off for a pint," announced Pete, eyeing the pub door that had just opened.

"Oh," I replied, "It's too beautiful to be inside."

I walked to the end of the pier and sat in the sunshine, dangling my feet above the crystal clear water. What to do for a couple of hours or so? I knew that once Pete was in the pub with his mates, it would be a job to drag him away. Then an idea came to me. On the deck of our boat was a rather scruffy old Canadian type canoe. I often used it at home paddling round the bays and inlets and was able to slide quietly amongst skerries and watch seals up close. It was very light and was constructed of a rubberised canvas stretched over a light wooden frame. The rubber was some-what perished and it was adorned with various patches and waterproof Elastoplast, which needed renewing frequently, but it was still reasonably sea worthy.

I lowered it over the side of the boat and pulled the narrow craft from the pier onto the beach where I could slip into it. A small wash gurgled from under the bows as I paddled strongly away from the shore. Under the surface, fronds of kelp waved in the gentle current. Far below I could see star fish and sea urchins festooned on the shadowy boulders. The pier and the village were behind me now and the water below me dark. The sun made the tiny wavelets sparkle and the intense light was hot on my face. What a stunning day. I stopped paddling well out into the bay and let my fingers trail in the water. Somewhere in the village a dog barked, the sound echoing and distorting as it reached my ears across the water. The only other sound was the water chuckling under the bows. After quite a while of soaking up the sun, I picked up my paddle again and gently and lazily dug into the calm water. I would paddle across the bay parallel with the village to the islands on the far side and look for seals. I might even try my fishing darra, thrown in off the deck at the last moment. It was too early for mackerel, but who knew what I might catch. I dipped the darra up and down in the deep still water and sat back, supplicating myself to the sun's rays.

Suddenly, nearby, I heard a strange sound. It was like a horse blowing through its nostrils. That's daft I thought. There's nothing out here. I know there are legends about kelpies, or water horses that lure maidens into the deep forever, but really! Then it came again, just behind me. I craned my neck round to try and see something. Suddenly, a black shape with a shiny fin crested out of the water and then another and another. It was a school of porpoises and the strange sound I had heard was the noise they made as they exhaled breath each time they surfaced. What a wonderful sight to see them so close. I grabbed my paddle and tried to keep up with them as they cruised past and for a brief moment they were alongside my canoe. I could almost touch them. As each one rose in their cartwheel of movement, they would expel breath in that horse like "hhrumph" noise. I was making a fine wake and tried to keep up with them. They were soon gone, far ahead of me and I was just left with a lovely memory.

Thinking about that day with the porpoises, I am reminded of a funny tale that happened in that very bay one breezy Saturday afternoon. I wasn't there to witness the events, so I hope my facts are correct, but was told about it with great relish later.

Most Saturdays, especially during the summer months, the lifeboat would leave harbour to run the engines and do some drill. Sometimes wives and girlfriends of the crew would be invited along for the ride. That particular Saturday the blue and orange lifeboat arrived in the bay with a brisk wind tumbling short steep waves against the shore. A rubber dinghy was lowered over the side and several people clambered aboard. They were going to be whizzed around the bay before the exercise continued with a visit to the village. Everyone had to be wearing a regulation lifeboat jacket and one buxom young lady somehow had a radio transmitter attached to hers. The lifeboat radios all operate on a special channel directly linked to the shore based coastguard.

The small craft bounced from wave to wave and delighted screams could be heard from onboard and on the shore. As the dinghy sped onwards, its occupants were shaken backwards and forwards and on every wave, the bosom of the well-endowed bonny lady must have pressed the transmit button of the radio.

"Oh, faster, faster," she squealed in glee, her voice being transmitted straight into the calm and disciplined coastguard office. This carried on for a short while before the radio on the lifeboat came to life.

"Lifeboat, what IS going on?' asked a stern, imperious voice from the coastguard.

Chapter Twenty-Two

No One Just Pops in for Tea

What a lovely June day it was. The loch shimmered under the bright sunlight and a gentle breeze embraced the new growth of grass in the meadow. The surrounding hills were green and the occasional, little puffy cloud floated across the blue sky. It seemed an ideal day to work in my vegetable garden. Rows of peas and broad beans were well up and there were trays of seedling lettuce, brassicas and leeks in my mini greenhouse. I had previously been down into the wood and gathered armfuls of fallen birch twigs, which would support the peas as they grew. With this job in mind and the few household chores finished, I was on my way out of the back door when the radio crackled in the corner of the kitchen.

"Caolas, Caolas, are you there?" a voice called. I recognised it as my friend, Mary in the estate office at the village.

"Just caught me," I replied.

"Some friends of yours are up on holiday in town and have sourced our phone number to try and get in contact with you. They would like to just pop down and visit you. Can you fetch them?"

That would entail a three hour round trip with the boat just to fetch them in.

"Who is it?" I asked. The thought of gently pottering about in my garden all day was fading fast.

"Maggie and Doug," was her reply.

"Can you tell them I'm on my way," I said delightedly.

We had known this couple for years and for some time they had been near neighbours when we lived down south.

It was a delightful morning to motor down the loch. Cormorants were busy fishing in the calm waters, their bodies glistening greeny black in the bright sunlight. A small raft of brilliant black and white eider drakes splashed away as we approached, their ducks no doubt either sitting on eggs or with young fluffy ducklings by now. What a beautiful day to show our old friends the magic place where we lived. They obviously had no idea how isolated our cottage was.

There were great hugs and embraces when we met on the pier, for Pete and I had not seen them in several years.

"You will not just be popping down for a cup of tea; you will be staying overnight," we informed them.

Maggie's mum was along with them and we hoped that an elderly lady would be able to climb out of the boat into the squashy dinghy back at moorings. We needn't have worried; she coped very well. The voyage back was full of laughter and joy. It was so lovely to see them again. They were amazed by the isolation of our abode, intrigued that we had a generator for our electricity and that we had no phone or road. The magnificence of the surrounding countryside took their breath away as they viewed up the loch to the cirque of high mountains that guarded the head of it. We took them into our new cottage and a great evening followed. We reminisced about the past and we learnt how their life had panned out since we had last met. They wanted to know all about our way of living, which was a world away from what they knew down in the South of England. We feasted on roast Caolas pork with lashings of crunchy crackling, washed down with plentiful quantities of homemade wine. The tales continued well into the night.

Much later as I lay in bed in the half light of an early dawn, I heard a snipe drumming just behind the house. What a perfect time it had been.

We awoke to another pristine morning. Maggie and I enjoyed our first cup of coffee sitting together in the warm sunlight on the doorstep. The sun had been long up and the warmth embraced us as we enjoyed the solitude.

"Aren't you ever lonely?" she quizzed.

No, I was never lonely, but was sometimes frightened. She would not have believed me if I told her how terrible the weather could be and how, from this very spot, we had often seen huge waves funnel through the narrows, pitching the poor boat at moorings, so that we would worry all night about its safety. No, today was for treating our friends to the idyllic side of our life there.

We carried out the kitchen table and chairs onto the grass in front of the house and I cooked a full breakfast for everyone. Piles of bacon, tomatoes, sausages, mushrooms and richly yoked eggs from our hens were served as the tide race swept past and the sunlight glinted off the loch. Too soon it was time to take them back to port and we hoped that they had enjoyed their brief experience of Caolas. I now know that they did, for twenty years later the image is still fresh in Maggie's mind.

Chapter Twenty-Three

Hay Making

With the cottage completely finished and work only just starting on the old house, we had a bit of spare time on our hands. It seemed a good idea to make some hay out of the front meadow for winter feed for the ponies. We had a tractor and mower, a hay turner, or 'Wuffler' as was printed on its side and a green baling machine. These had all been purchased by us and brought down to Caolas when we first arrived.

Many years previously, the people living at Caolas had made hay for their beasts, cutting the grass with scythes, but nothing had been done with the meadow for countless years. It had grown up every summer, died down in the winter and was full of wild flowers. The delicate blue harebells were now out and the grass was just seeding; the ideal time to cut for hay.

We followed the weather forecast avidly for a week or so as it rained continuously, but at last there was a brighter spell expected. The mower was greased and the tractor filled from cans of red diesel, which we had brought in by boat. I watched as Pete set off into the field and lowered the mower. Long grass and flowers fell in a silvery sheen behind him as he made his first pass 'round the meadow. We didn't think that anyone had ever cut the grass mechanically there before. The powerful turbo mower with new blades was making an excellent job and swathes of grass lay neatly on the ground. All the time the sun beat strongly down and in a couple of hours the entire field was cut.

"There will be plenty of keep for the winter in that lot," Pete commented as he stepped down off the tractor. It would need a day of drying before taking the Wuffler in to turn it. We both agreed that it would be so lovely not to have to transport all the winter hay in by boat. There was something satisfying about making our own.

The next day dawned cloudless again and by lunchtime Pete inspected the cut grass by scuffing some with his foot. The Wuffler was attached to the tractor and he set off into the field to fluff it all up. I followed with a two pronged hay fork to tease out the tangled heavy bits. Where the grass was thin it was already drying well and the pollen rose in clouds. My arms and legs were becoming tanned as I worked away in shorts and a skimpy top. That evening a large, orange, sun set, boding well for the following day.

Once the dew had dried by mid morning, we were out turning again, spreading it out and then pulling it back into lines before evening.

"I think it will bale tomorrow," Pete stated, as he bent and picked up a handful of soft hay and scrunched it in his hands. There had been a warm breeze all day, which had helped to dry it out. It smelt wonderful and had maintained its pale green colour. It was going to be top quality hay.

More wuffling by late morning had shaken out the remains of the dew and the ready hay was turned into neat rows. The baler was attached to the tractor. We were ready for our first haymaking at Caolas. With huge anticipation we had a quick lunch and I followed Pete out to the tractor to take photos. How many bales would we make? We hoped to bale and cart the crop in to the barn before nightfall.

I watched as he made his way around the outside of the field, with the rhythmic drumming of the baler as it devoured piles of hay, compressed them, tied them and purged them out of the back of the machine to lay in neat rectangles at intervals around the meadow. I clicked away with my camera, for this was a momentous occasion. The tractor was coming towards me again, almost around the field for the first time, when there was a loud bang and the regular beat of the baler stopped. One of the shear pins must have gone. I knew that if there was a blockage, or a piece of metal was swept up into the baling chamber, these shear pins act like a safety valve and by fracturing they shut down the mechanism and avoided damaging the machine. They were easily replaced and we had a bag of them in the barn. Pete was off the tractor and had the lid of the baler up. Before I reached him, I could hear the expletives. I knew that he was very tense as the lunch time forecast had indicated an area of low pressure was moving into western Scotland and we had to get this hay in before it spoilt.

"Drive chain broken; the whole thing is buggered," he grumbled dejectedly.

I peered into the baler. What a mess. The main chain, that sets the sequence and drives the whole thing from the tractor power take off, had broken and set off a catalogue of catastrophic breakages. The machine is very accurately timed for each part to work without clashing and once the chain had broken the timing became random. I could see that the large metal grabs that help compress the hay were broken and the curved needles that are threaded with baler twine were bent at right angles. The knife was also broken and the rod that carries the knotting mechanism was sheared. It was indeed buggered. All our hopes of getting the hay in were lost. The parts for the baler could not be purchased locally and indeed we would probably have to order them from the manufacturer down in England.

If we went by boat now up to the village, we would just be in time to make some phone calls before the offices shut. Maybe parts could be sourced and sent up within a few days. The boat journey seemed to take ages, rowing out, striking up the boat, casting off moorings and then six miles at nine knots. If only it would go faster.

The supplier who sold us the baler was contacted and he supplied the manufacturer's number. Luckily, Pete was able to phone them directly. Yes, the parts would be dispatched the following morning by Data post and should arrive in twenty four hours. All we could do now was to wait.

The clouds rolled in that night and a gentle drizzle fell. We had fetched in the twenty bales before dark and retired very discontentedly to bed. The next day the rain fell unceasingly all day and the following day the mail boat arrived without the parts. They had obviously not arrived in time for the sailing.

We fetched the parts from the post office in port the day after and on a damp, midge-infested evening, Pete started to replace the broken parts. It was pure hell. The midges bit and buzzed in our ears as we worked together. I was passing tools, rather like a nurse helping a surgeon with a tricky operation. Once he had replaced all the broken bits, there was the tricky job of timing the machine again. My job was to slowly turn the heavy flywheel by hand as Pete set up the component parts. Clouds of tiny flying beasties made a haze around our heads and anyone who has endured the Highland midge knows what agony we were in. The timing of the machine had to be dead accurate and yet again I had to try and turn the large flywheel. At long last, just as dark was descending and the rain was becoming heavier, we finished the job.

The machine was ready to roll again, but what about the weather? Well, it rained more or less continuously every day for a fortnight and gradually our lovely hay was flattened into a sodden mess. It was completely ruined and as the summer progressed it was gradually absorbed back into the meadow as fresh grass pushed up through it. There was no other option; we would have to ring up the hay merchant later in the autumn and pay the landing craft to bring us down the winter feed. The weather had beaten us again. Sometimes we were so disheartened.

Chapter Twenty-Four

A Visit to the Doctor

I had not been feeling well for some time. Frequent deep abdominal pains had plagued me for some months and I had joked that it was my appendix complaining about all the bags of cement I had lifted. Walking helped palliate the pain and I spent long days up in the hills behind Caolas, but the agonising pain soon returned. It was obviously time to pay a call to the doctor and obtain a professional diagnosis.

The doctor came to the village by mail boat the following Wednesday morning and I was waiting on the pier when the boat arrived. The doctor was a tall distinguished looking gentleman dressed in a tweed suit and he gently guided me into the office of the estate, which doubled up as a doctor's surgery.

After I explained where the pain was, he thought it would be a good idea to examine and palpate my stomach. The tatty Venetian blind was pulled down, although it did not completely cover the window and the light was switched on. I was instructed to lie on the floor as there was no examining couch. He kindly placed his tweed trilby on the floor beneath my head and vigorously rubbed his cold hands together before proceeding with the examination.

I was aware that anyone walking by outside could peer in and see me with my midriff exposed, prostrate on the floor. I could hear other waiting patients jostling in the small hallway outside the "surgery" door.

"Hmm, I'm not happy with this," he commented, as I doubled up with pain.

"You live right up the loch don't you?"

I nodded mutely and stood up as he strode across the room to the telephone.

"Hospital for you," he stated as he dialled a number.

"I can't," I wailed. "I have my boat outside."

I tried protesting that my husband was six miles up the loch without a boat and that I didn't have my nightie and wash bag with me. He wasn't taking any notice. The door was opened and the small gathering of people outside, who had probably heard every word, were approached for help. Yes, Sarah would lend me nightwear and a flannel and Tam would run me into port and then take the boat back to Caolas. All were very concerned. What lovely friends I had.

As Tam and I went down the loch in the boat, the outcome of my visit to the doctor struck home. I hadn't expected to have to go to hospital. I was supposed to be working. We had a busy schedule to adhere to. I had completed the plans for the old house renovation and we had started work stripping the old roof off. Maybe I would only be in for the weekend for observation, I thought, as I caught the train to the hospital, which was fifty miles away.

Following a huge operation, it was five weeks before I was finally released from hospital. Even then, I was not allowed to go home as it was deemed far too remote. I stayed with friends for a couple of weeks in the fishing port while I convalesced, before being allowed back to lovely Caolas. I had been so homesick in hospital.

I was happy to be home, but exhausted, as Barney greeted me with exuberant licks. He must have thought I had gone forever. All heavy lifting was banned for months, so Pete meanwhile had tried to carry on working on his own. It must have been so difficult for him. Our employer suggested that he brought in a couple of workers to live at Caolas during the week and keep the work going.

Everything had changed for me at Caolas. I was no longer part of the work team. These strangers were staying in my home and I would have to cook for them. Since I had returned, my role was suddenly diminished to tea lady and housewife. I suddenly felt so weak, helpless and desperately unhappy. My poor body was battered and fragile. I was feeling very sorry for myself. The work was progressing at the house and I was no longer any part of it. My plans lay in the kitchen and yet nobody talked to me about the building.

Pete was enjoying the male camaraderie and every evening they sat down after supper to drink beer and watch a men's "blood and snot" video brought in from town. My home was no longer my own. I would often sit in the kitchen with the dog while the drinking and the gore on the telly continued in the lounge. What was happening? I didn't fit into this scene at all.

I was also frightened and apprehensive. Pete seemed to have successfully conquered a drink problem he had when we lived in England, yet this was starting to reappear. I wished I could talk to a girlfriend, who would probably put it all in perspective, but to talk to Jeannie on the radio was out of the question with most of the fishing fleet probably listening in.

For the first time since we had been at Caolas, I was surrounded by people and yet I felt lonely. I knew that the workers would have to stay for several months at least. I would just have to get used to the situation. It was impossible for Pete to cope with all the work on his own. They were decent, clean chaps, so I really couldn't grumble. Until I was fit to work again on the house, I would have to be "the little woman indoors". Oh boy, did that rankle with me!

We would take the workers back to port on a Friday morning and fetch them in again on a Monday morning. That is, if there wasn't a gale!

Weekends became special, as we were on our own.

Chapter Twenty-Five

Rough Voyage

"Malin, Hebrides, Storm force 10 imminent," announced the calm voice of the shipping forecast lady. I groaned and turned over to switch off the radio. It was still completely dark outside and I curled up deeper in my bed. Not another storm. It was mid January and we seemed to have been plagued by a close succession of Atlantic low pressures racing in to thrash western Scotland.

When I had fetched the workers in on Monday, I had left Pete in port as he had to go off on business for our employer.

I was feeling much stronger and starting to do light work in the house, but I still needed a hand to moor up the boat to the heavy chain. It was now Wednesday and I was beginning to worry about getting the workers out on Friday and collecting Pete again. A friend in the village had recently said that in the winter it was a miracle to achieve anything in the short days and the gales and every day was taken up with routine jobs. I could only agree.

The first drops of heavy rain battered against the kitchen window as I made a cup of coffee. Thank goodness the roof of the old house had been completed and the men were starting work demolishing the inside. After clearing the breakfast dishes and tidying the kitchen, I fought my way against the stinging hail stones and strengthening wind across the meadow and into the house. A radio was blaring out pop music and sounds of heavy hammering were coming from deep within the interior.

"Tea up," I shouted, above the cacophony of sound as I trod gingerly across the detritus of a recently felled wall. The men were edgy and anxious when I told them about the weather forecast and both wanted out on the Thursday if there was a lull after this storm. They wanted to get back to their families for the weekend.

Huge, wind-driven waves pounded up the loch all day and incessant rain drove against the two houses. This storm seemed set to go on longer. I switched on my alarm again for the early forecast the next morning, but was awake well before it went off. I was very worried about taking the boat out in stormy weather.

The portable radio hissed and crackled. It was a weather forecast man this time and he started with the outlook all down the east coast of Britain; "Tyne, Dogger..."

"Oh please hurry up!" I cried.

I waited as he got to Irish Sea; so near now and the signal was fading.

"Malin, Hebrides, storm force 10, south westerly dropping to Force 7 before backing north westerly and increasing to storm force 10 again."

"Bloody hell, what a horrible forecast," I sighed.

"It's today or who knows when," I informed the workers over breakfast.

The wind had certainly dropped a little, although the dark clouds still seemed to be scudding past. The men were more than keen to get out and went to pack up their clothes. I was not going to take Barney with me on what looked like being quite a dangerous trip. There would not be any room in the wheelhouse for a large dog and I knew how much he hated boats. I set him down plenty of food and water, just in case I couldn't get back that night and ran my hands through his black and tan fur.

"Poor old lad; I've got to leave you again."

I realised I was shaking at the prospect of a rough trip. He picked up on my emotion and, whining softly, he nuzzled my hand.

The boat at moorings was sitting fairly calmly. The tide was out and the waves had exhausted their fury on the beach at the other side of the shingle spit. I completed engine checks and ran it up for a while to warm it up. We lashed all the empty diesel drums securely at each side of the deck. They would have to be filled in port. The boat hook was tied down and satisfied that all was secure, I cast off.

I am not a religious person, but I hoped that God would forgive my very long abstinence that morning as I sent up a silent prayer for our safety.

The middle loch was rough, but I knew it would be nothing to what we would experience once around the point.

"Hold on," I shouted, as I swung the wheel and the boat came 'round into the outer loch. It was as if all hell was let loose. Immediately, the boat lunged into a huge trough of green water. It was the sort of wave that makes you wonder whether you will keep on submerging and never come up the other side. I knew it was dangerous to keep full power on while in such a steep trough, as you could take a heap of water over the bow. I eased back the Teleflex and the power dropped away momentarily. The sea immediately ahead was creaming and tumbling over in cascades of white water.

I knew from looking at the sounder in the past that the loch was very shallow there, where there was a hard lip of rock left over from the ice age. This caused any sea to pile up in dangerous, short sharp waves. I powered on again and we laboriously made our way forward against the turbulent sea. I tried to keep out in mid channel, which was probably rougher because of the angle of the wind, but we were further from the jagged cliffs if anything went wrong with the engine. I still had vivid memories of the old engine. The sea was as ferocious as that which I had experienced eighteen months previously on the night rescue, only then I was on a much larger boat.

As we left the influence of the shallow water and made our way into the outer loch, the waves became much larger and longer. The gale had raged for over twenty four hours and instead of the usual short choppy sea that we often ploughed into on our way to port, this was a whole new experience. The waves were not breaking ahead of us now; they were just huge troughs and ridges. I just kept the power on and we would frequently drop into a trough where you could see nothing but green water. The wave would race past and we would climb out onto the crest again. The dark wet rock of the cliffs and islands could be seen for a moment before we plunged back down into another green hole. I braced myself and held onto the wheel with white knuckled hands. It was frightening, but strangely exhilarating as we rollercoasted on.

The distance that normally took twenty minutes on a calm day was taking much longer. Nobody spoke. We were approaching the most dangerous part of the trip where I had to turn broadside to the wind and waves. Many boats in the past had been swept onto the sharp rocks of the point just before the safety of the harbour.

"Oh, engine keep on going," I prayed.

Thank goodness the waves were not tumbling over in crests, or we might have been swamped. There were just a few more yards of sickening lurching and then we were safe. The harbour walls cocooned us from the fury outside. It was only then I realised what a grip I had on the wheel as my hands were frozen shut.

Pete had also heard the forecast in port and wondered if we might try to come out before the next gale was due. Apparently, he had come down to the harbour to see most of the boats tied up. The big ferry was also not running and as he was turning to go back up the street, he met one of the well- known fishermen.

"Your bloody missus won't be coming out in that fucking wee boat," the man stated. They were both watching flumes of water break over the harbour wall and sheltering by the fish market.

"Well fuck me," he spluttered. "That's your bloody boat coming 'round the point now." His language was always colourful.

A broad grin broke out on my face as I came alongside the steps and Pete came down to tie up the ropes.

"You are completely mad," he expostulated, but he was grinning too.

No, we didn't get back to Barney that night. We were offered a couple of berths aboard the landing craft tied up at the pier, but the incessant noise of boats grinding against each other kept us awake. The storm had abated enough the following morning for us to make a run for home.

Chapter Twenty-Six

Cars

"I've got a new car coming soon," announced Johnny proudly, as we added another strip of insulating tape and secured it with a jubilee clip to his decaying brake fluid pipe.

"Not before time," I muttered darkly through chattering teeth, as I cast an eye over the expanse of moorland and worked out the equation of hours of daylight left versus miles to walk back to the village if necessary.

"That's better," he muttered, wiping his hands on the verge before gently lowering the bonnet down. Well, he dare not drop it because the hinges had almost rusted away and any impact could cause the wings, or what was left of them, to sag even further. As it was, a few flakes of rust had collected on the road.

It was one dark, winter day and on a trip up from Caolas to the village, Johnny had kindly offered to drive me the eight miles of tarmac road to visit friends who lived on the other side of the peninsula. This stretch of road only ran between the two villages and was not connected to the national network of roads.

At the time that I lived there, if anyone wanted a car to run about on this eight mile highway, all one had to do was to go to the nearest MOT testing garage, forty minutes away by boat and then twenty minutes by road. One would then choose the best runner from the yard full of MOT failures. Usually, it was the most recent one as some had subsided there for years. For a small fee, the garage would trailer it back to town where a crane would lower it onto a waiting barge. It was then towed for forty minutes, or more if it was a rough day, back to the village where a makeshift ramp onto the beach allowed the vehicle to be offloaded onto the rocky shore. The car would then be dragged unceremoniously up the beach onto the road by the local tractor. Then it was ready to start the last months of its life bumping along rough tracks, or the better, but still uncomfortable eight miles between villages. Nobody paid road tax or insurance, unobtainable without an MOT.

Johnny's new car would not be a pristine little number straight out of a showroom, showing the latest registration. His next car would be the choice of runners from "death row". Given the number of times his motors took to the hills and ditches, usually at about 11.30pm on a Saturday night, the average lifespan for a Johnny-mobile would be six months.

There also was another novel, little car that Pete and I had the honour of owning for trips when we were up at the village. This designer model was articulated, an obvious advantage considering the steep bends above the village. Its makers in the Ruhr valley hadn't created it that way, but in the autumn of its existence the back axle had somehow parted company with the rest of the vehicle; the west coast disease, some would say. Something to do with being marinated for at least three hundred and twenty days a year in acid rain, not to mention a fair bit of salt spindrift whipped up from the bay to boot.

An engineer of vision had solved the problem by passing a length of creel rope through a convenient rust hole in the floor, around the axle and back to be tightened and secured with a Spanish windlass to the seat mounting on the driver's side of the car. This vehicle had a preponderance for wandering on the road, unnervingly usually when approaching another vehicle, or coming down the steep hill into the village. The offside driver's wheel had been filched off Sandy's abandoned car at the village tip. It was not a good match as only two studs fitted, the rest having been sawn off to accommodate the wheel, so there was a hint of a wobble.

The other distracting feature of this conveyance was that the driver's door wouldn't stay shut. A piece of baler twine tied between the remains of the door handle and the steering column helped to lessen the incidents of the door flying open on sharp left hand bends, but it was still dodgy.

I remember one day offering to take two collie dogs and a full gas cylinder from the pier to the big house. The car creaked somewhat under load and I had only gone half a mile when there was a hot rubbery smell. I got out and peered underneath to try and trace the source of the overheating only to find that the old car had finally collapsed under the extra weight and the rusty red body lay heavily on the tyres. It was the end of an era. It had added another dimension to creative driving.

A recently deceased car still had churned up mud all over it, suggesting that the driver and passengers had tramped around it trying to diagnose its final ailment. This was often accompanied by the muddy imprint of a size ten welly aimed somewhere on the abandoned body as a parting shot.

Farm and croft yards all over the Highlands are final homes to family cars going back over the ages, such as Ford Anglias and Vauxhall Victors. I'd even seen a little old grey Austin A30 lying peacefully alongside an old Landrover and baling machine.

When bracken fronds unfurl out of where a bonnet used to be, the car takes on monument status. By then it is maybe just a shell, with any working parts going on to do service in current vehicles. Lucas, the component manufacturer, have no idea of the concept of interchangeable parts unless they come up to the Highlands. Some shells have gone on to do duty as dog kennels and chicken houses and I did see one very tasteful Volvo estate filled with growbags and producing a bumper crop of tomatoes.

Chapter Twenty-Seven

The Dancing Lights

"While sailing a little south of the Plata on one very dark night, the sea presented a wonderful and most beautiful spectacle. There was a fresh breeze, and every part of the surface, which during the day is seen as foam, now glowed with a pale light. The vessel drove before her bows two billows of liquid phosphorus, and in her wake she was followed by a milky train. As far as the eye reached, the crest of every wave was bright, and the sky above the horizon, from the reflected glare of these livid flames, was not so utterly obscure as over the vault of the heavens."

Charles Darwin, Chapter VIII, *The Voyage of the Beagle*, December 1833

Millions of stars filled the deep night sky as we made our way back down to the beach. There was no moon, but the mountain tops with their covering of snow were etched against this starlight display.

We had been visiting our neighbours, Jeannie and Iain, six miles up at the head of the loch and late in the evening we all strolled down the path from their house. It was March and our breath rose in clouds on that crisp, magical night. They waved us goodbye as we rowed in the dinghy out to our boat on one of their moorings. It would be easy to see our way home down the loch with this ethereal light. There was no wind at all and the loch looked deep, still and dark. I looked back as we motored and marvelled at the cirque of magnificent mountains that guarded the head of the loch. A favourite mountain with its sharply pointed summit looked ghostly silver.

My eye was then distracted by our wake. At nine knots we churned out a fair wash and tonight this was a stunning white blue, visible against the deep black for many yards behind the boat. It was phosphorescence, nature's brilliant light show.

The phosphorescence, or more correctly bioluminescence, that we saw that evening is produced from single celled organisms called dinoflagellates, which use the sun's energy for photosynthesis like plants. They are made of armoured cellulose and use two appendages to help them move actively. When you stir up the water, the electrons in their atoms absorb energy and give it off as light.

This prosaic explanation didn't detract from the unexpected beauty that these dancing lights in the water gave. All the way home the ghostly light followed us while, above in the heavens, the Plough to our right and Orion's belt to our left guided our way. We switched off the navigation lights on the boat and cruised along in complete darkness. There would be nobody else around at this time of night. The entrance to the narrows was very dark and we made our way carefully, aware of the big skerry just off to our left. Pete shone his torch on the shiny dangerous reef as we passed. The tide was nearly slack and the water calm as we slid alongside our mooring.

What a lovely evening it had been. Good company and food, calm weather for a change and then nature's luminous fiesta. The phosphorescence still danced from the oar tips as we rowed ashore.

It was too beautiful an evening to go straight in. I splashed around in my wellies in the water just off the beach, fascinated with the tiny pin pricks of light that I created. As I swirled my hands in the cold water, it was like firework night sparklers. It was mesmerising and I was not aware how long I stayed out on the beach. Pete had long gone in to attend to more earthly chores like stoking up the Rayburn.

A wet black nose nuzzled into my cold hands and I realised Barney had come out to the beach to find me.

"Come on old fellow," I said, as I fondled his head. "Let's go to bed."

Chapter Twenty-Eight

Prospecting

I had all Saturday to myself. What a treat. We had taken out the workers on the Friday afternoon after a busy week and Pete and I were having a long awaited day off. At long last I was fit enough to be back on the building team and in between cooking meals I managed to put in a few hours each day working in the interior of the old house

I suggested a walk that morning, but Pete pulled a face. I had already thought that he would be much happier pottering around at home. It was early May and as so often happened in Western Scotland, we had a run of beautiful, clear, sunny days. I packed a "piece" for my lunch and stuffed my waterproofs in my day bag just as a precaution in case the weather changed. Camera, map and compass were also included. I had it in my mind to walk up to the long abandoned Mica mines high up in the hills behind Caolas. Barney was no longer able to climb on rough ground, so reluctantly I left the old dog at home.

Tiny, vivid blue milkworts dotted my path as I walked around the beach side of the old meadow. We were hoping to try and make hay again that summer and already there was the start of new green growth over the whole meadow. Another job drew my attention as I skirted the shore. There was quite a lot of plastic detritus washed up on the sand. In spite of living so far up an uninhabited loch, rubbish would wash in with the tides and wind. I tried to keep this lovely beach free of polypropylene ropes and washing up bottles by collecting them up and burying them in the hole where we dumped the household rubbish. It still wasn't the ideal solution, but my only other option would be to burn it all and that would release noxious smoke into the atmosphere.

I walked on to the end of the shore where I climbed over the steep headland and into the next bay. I was still not completely fit and the exertion made me puff. I sat on a large rock and looked out to the small island just offshore. An otter family lived there, but I had not seen them for some time. A bit more of a climb and I dropped into Horseshoe bay. A small burn gurgled down from the corrie above and spent itself on the rocky beach. I remembered trying to cross this burn in spate one winter's day during the first year we were at Caolas and misjudging my jump. I landed very wetly before the far bank. The memory made me smile, although at the time I had very wet legs for the remainder of the day.

Onwards along the shore, it wasn't long before I spied the remains of an old stone and concrete jetty jutting out into the water. This landing place had been constructed to offload goods and machinery for the mica mine. There was also the concrete base of a long-gone shed, which had been used for rough dressing the mined Mica before it was shipped out. The mineral Mica had been discovered high up in the hills behind me in 1938 by the Geological Survey of Great Britain. Due to the heavy loss of ships in the Atlantic during the Second World War, the transportation of Mica that normally came from India was severely disrupted. The mine had been worked during World War II to extract the mineral. Mica was mainly used in the production of radios.

My track now led uphill away from the shore. On journeys up the loch in the boat, I had espied from far out the remains of a zig zag track cutting up the steep hillside. It would only be possible to follow this track in winter and early spring before the dense bracken obliterated the way. The young bracken was only just unfolding in tight crosier-like heads as I advanced up. Now and again I found the remains of a track, mainly on the switch backs where the stone had been built up. This amazing path was constructed by troops who were training in the area at the beginning of World War II and every bit of machinery would have to have been loaded on ponies at the jetty and hauled up the mountain side and the blasted and quarried mica brought down.

It was a relentless uphill trek and I made several stops to catch my breath. A jumble of hills to the south came into view across the loch, fading into a nebulous bluey-purple horizon. When about halfway up the steep hillside, I noticed on the map that it showed a dwelling, but when I reached the spot there were only weather bleached old planks of wood scattered around, the remains of a large shed. Maybe that was the accommodation for the miners?

The sun warmed my back as I pushed on upwards. The path had disappeared and I made my way over increasingly rocky ground. Far up and ahead I could see the whole end of a ridge glinting in the strong sun light; the mica mine spoil heap. I was nearly there. I could only imagine the discomfort that those miners had to endure, stomping up that hillside on cold wet winter days. There were shards of transparent mica everywhere on the ground. I picked up a piece and peeled off wafer thin layers. There were large old iron pipes laid up the ridge. They must have been from a compressor to work the machinery that mined out the mica. There were no tunnels into the hillside; the mining was all done on the surface.

The rock lay in inclined bands of white pegmatite and grey schist. I moved up further and came to an old roofless stone building. It was constructed from schist, but the method of construction was more like buildings seen in the Lake District than the West Highland way. It was beautifully constructed of flat stones all interlocked. Maybe the builder of this substantial building had been a Lakeland man. Inside was a huge compressor, still intact but abandoned after the end of the war. It must have taken many ponies to haul this behemoth to the top of a mountain. Fancy trying to start it on a damp winter's day, I mused. Did they have "Easy Start" in those days?

Sitting eating my "piece" in the warm sunshine, I noticed some small white rocks nearby. They were almost quartz and had a peppering of dull red garnets on their surfaces. They were beautiful and I collected several for my stone collection. Garnets are semi-precious and I hoped to find a big one that I could tease out of the rock to make into a necklace. I wondered how they would polish up in a lapidary machine.

There was a big corrie behind the mine and a jewel of a lochan nestled in its bowl. A large herd of deer were moving nonchalantly across the flanks of the mountain, the puffy clouds making passing shadows on the bleached old grass. I fancied a swim in those dark waters and I clambered down to its shores and stripped off and waded in. Oh, was it cold, but refreshing. The deer looked down and noted my presence, but they were far enough away not to be bothered. I only splashed around for a few minutes before hauling myself out onto the warm rocks on the shore.

With some mica and a few garnet rocks in my bag, I started back down the long route to the shore. There were no boats on the loch and I had not seen another person all day, so isolated was that spot. Sometime later, I reached our cottage again, tired but elated by my gem discovery. I arranged the stones with others I had collected previously on the kitchen window sill and to this day, I still have the garnets in their stones.

Chapter Twenty-Nine

The Women's Pool

I crouched low behind the bucking bow of the inflatable dinghy as it sped up the loch. On every other wave a quantity of salty green water landed heavily in my lap. This was my taxi for the day. We were going to have a girls' day out to fish the river and I had high hopes of bringing back a tasty morsel for supper.

Jeannie, my good friend and neighbour from the head of the loch six miles away, had radioed earlier that she was coming to fetch me. I could hear the whine of a powerful outboard as I had stood waiting on the beach. The craft speedily entered the narrows and all I could see was her head sticking up above the rubber bow. She appeared to be lying out along the bottom of the boat and steering with her feet. Seemingly, at the last minute, she threw herself backwards and killed the engine. The large rubber boat crunched heavily up on the shore.

"Phew, that was fun," she laughed, brushing her hair back from her face. She explained that she had to lie out flat in the inflatable boat to distribute some of the weight, because when she had opened up the engine in the bay in front of her house, the front of the craft had risen alarmingly and obliterated her view.

As a passenger on the way back, my function was to provide a bit of weight to keep the front down. She didn't spare the engine either and we were charging along at about twenty knots. Luckily, I had donned waterproofs for the trip and each time a flood of water came on board, my other function

was to bail it out with an old plastic mug. We grinned idioti-
cally at each other.

In no time at all we were back ashore and sitting in her
living room warming our hands on steaming mugs of coffee
before we set out up the river. A box of fishing gear lay on
the floor and we sorted out the necessary rods for a good
day's sport.

The Argo, which is an eight-wheeled, all terrain vehicle,
seemed the quickest way to transport us and the gear up the
valley to the pool she had chosen and we loaded everything
onboard. They are not the most comfortable of conveyances
and I cradled the rods and tried to hang on as we jolted and
bumped up the barely discernable track. Bushes at the side
swiped spitefully at our faces and every few feet the huge-
tyred wheels would drop into holes and the mud would spit
out in a viscous brown fountain behind us, as the vehicle
clambered on. Jeannie was enjoying herself and gunned the
Argo on as unceasingly as she had the Rubba Dubba.

We seemed to have travelling eternally up the deep valley
when she stopped the vehicle and announced that we had
arrived. I hobbled laboriously after her, wondering if my
vertebrae would ever recover from the pounding. We were
pushing our way through deep bracken and I was aware that
the wind had died away completely. Thank goodness the sun
was shining brightly, otherwise we would have been harassed
by droves of biting midges.

"Sssh," Jeannie hissed and put up her hand to stop me. She
silently extended the rod and tied the spinner on with a fisherman's knot. We crouched in the high foliage and she whispered what I was to do. This was the famous corner pool and
large fish lurked in the depths.

"Your first cast must be the best," she instructed. "Creep

out on to the flat rock and cast to the far side of the pool and you will probably get a fish."

"Some chance," I thought. My prowess for fishing was pretty abysmal, other than catching the suicidal mackerel in the loch. I crept forward, trying to keep the fishing hook from snagging the tough bracken stems. Suddenly, ahead of me, I saw a large flat rock and the deep pool beyond. Carefully, I extricated the sharp hook from myself and the shaft of the rod, stood up and cast as far as I could over the silent, dark water. The spinner dropped with a loud splosh right across the pool under an ancient alder tree. I started to wind it in for another try, disappointed that I had not secured the famous first cast when, suddenly, I felt a huge tug on the rod. The line went taut and the rod bowed.

"I've got a fish!" I shouted, jumping on the spot, all attempts at silence shattered. Jeannie came swiftly through the bracken.

"Play it now, carefully," she advised.

I let the reel run out and started winding it in again. Gradually, I reeled in the fish. It would be awful to lose it now. Jeannie was waiting with the landing net. The fish was fighting boldly, its silver body breaking the surface of the water. So near now. We could see it was a large fish. She dipped in the net under its muscular body and lifted it out of the water.

"Wow, a big sea trout," she gasped. "What a beauty. Well done."

She hit it expertly with her wooden "priest" and it lay still on the rock, displaying its beautiful iridescent colours.

I had caught a fish and I was so amazed. On many occasions I had tried to catch the tiny trout that lived in the hill lochans and mostly failed.

"I think we have supper," I said.

It was Jeannie's turn now and because I had made such a noise over catching my fish, all the remaining fish had probably deserted the pool for somewhere quieter. We gave them a chance to settle, sat and ate our "piece" and leisurely languished in the warm sunshine. A while later, Jeannie carefully set her rod, stood up quietly and cast right out. The spinner dropped into the pool and immediately there was a swirl of water. Another fish. This was unbelievable, but she had said that this pool was notorious for yielding to the first cast. It was indeed another beautiful sea trout, not quite as large as mine, but it was quickly dispatched. We grinned at each other. What a fruitful and enjoyable day it had been.

The bracken parted and Jeannie's husband and the Ghillie, who was a lad on job training to become a fisherman and stalker, appeared by the poolside. They had come to try their hand at catching a fish and probably show the women how to do it. They cast and cast, all in vain. Not a thing stirred in that deep dark pool. In exasperation, the Ghillie even scrambled about on the bank and dug with his fingers to try and find a worm. The men were desperate. Manly honour was at stake. Our two sea trout lay resplendent in the fishing bag. The sun went down and the biting midges came out in clouds. Every paradise must have its flaw. Just one more attempt and we would go home.

There was absolutely no luck at all. It was certainly the women's victory that day. There was even talk by the males that the corner pool should be renamed the "Cailleach's" pool, which is Gaelic for old woman.

The two trout provided an excellent supper for us all.

Chapter Thirty

Ovine Interlude

A male ptarmigan rose vociferously just in front of me as I clambered up the last few yards to the top of the mountain. I had not been there for many months, the nearest large mountain to Caolas. Sitting down on the summit, I scanned the horizon. The islands out in the sound seemed to be almost floating above the luminous sea. On turning around and looking inland, I could see the outlines of hazy mountains disappearing into the distance. Warm sunshine played on my shoulders as I unpacked my lunch. There was hardly a breath of wind and I sat in quiet harmony with the views.

A movement just below the summit suddenly caught my eye. A light grey rock seemed to move. I blinked and focused on the spot. It was not a rock, but a sheep and then I spied several others sitting nearby. Now I knew there shouldn't be any sheep up there, because three years previously all the sheep had been rounded up and taken away when the estate was sold. I centred my binoculars on the group and saw some extremely woolly individuals. This group had obviously missed being gathered and had made their home high on the slopes of the mountain. They were real "roughies", or sheep that have not been sheared each year. Some looked like ancient discarded sofas as they lay sprawled on the short grass, with all the new growth of wool piling untidily out of the old grey fleeces. Apart from that they looked very healthy, despite having missed all the routine medication deemed necessary to keep a sheep healthy.

I left them to their leisurely perambulations and made my way back down the mountain. I decided to contact my friend and sheep farmer Lachie and ask if he was interested in gathering them for himself.

"Aye, we will take the dogs up and bring them back gently," he informed me when we met in the village some days later. A date was set and I fetched him in with our boat. Two working collie dogs came along too. One was an old and steady dog and the other a lively young bitch.

"The young one will find them and gather them up and the old one will bring them down quietly," Lachie informed me.

The dinghy crunched on to the beach at Caolas and the dogs leapt out exuberantly, their tongues hanging out like slices of ham. They were ready for the active day ahead. With day bags on our backs, we started up the large mountain. Lachie had a lifetime of walking in the hills and he set an easy pace. We talked on many diverse subjects as we climbed and the warm sunlight made the journey very enjoyable.

Pete was already up somewhere ahead on the range of mountains, as he and a stalker had set out much earlier for a day of deer stalking. The autumn stag season had started and there had been a deer seen during the summer with badly shaped antlers that needed culling, before he passed his genes to any more females.

Lachie's pace transported us seemingly without the greatest effort and we were high in the vast corrie when we spied the sheep through binoculars grazing far above us. We circled the corrie and made our way up to the summit ridge. The sheep were in almost the same place where I had seen them several weeks earlier.

Finding a large boulder, we sat down against it to have a

160

rest and eat our "pieces". The dogs flopped beside us, their eyes sparkling and their tongues lolling. A small brown Argos butterfly fluttered past and the only sound was of the gentle breeze caressing the grass. It would have been pleasant to just stay there and bask in the sun, but it was time to move again.

We were just about to stand up when we heard distant voices. Lachie put his finger to his lips and we stayed put. The voices came closer and we "keeked" out from our hidden position. Just below us we spied a pair of deerstalker hats bobbing past. Pete and his co-stalker were in deep and earnest conversation. We grinned to each other. Some good stalkers these were; they had no idea that we were just above them. Lachie whispered that he was very tempted to give his rutting deer rendition and I stifled a giggle at the thought.

"Wait 'til I tell them what great stalkers they are," he whispered.

They passed below us with no idea that two people and two dogs were hidden not twenty yards away. How amazing in that wild jumble of hills, that we had been so close to each other.

The men gone, we clambered to our feet. It was time to move the sheep. On an order, the young dog streaked off to the right. She had been weaving impetuously behind Lachie's heels since we started. We watched the sheep through binoculars as first one lifted her head, then another stamped her foot. The young dog circled them all through the deep undergrowth. She was out of sight for some minutes as she "lifted" all the sheep. Then, heavily laden sheep started to move forward, their enormous fleeces swaying as they ran. She brought them slithering down the steep slope to just above us. It was a virtuoso performance. We would now have to take them more slowly in such heat.

There was already the smell of hot wool in the air. Lachie called the young dog back and she obediently took up position behind our heels. The old dog took over and the sheep dropped to a walk.

We had a long way to go and the sun was moving 'round. Now and again we stopped and let them rest, as some were panting. One or two tried a bid for freedom again back up the hill, but were quickly stopped by the dogs. Deep heather and boulders impeded our progress, but eventually we arrived onto the flat ground behind Caolas. The dogs herded the recalcitrant sheep in the yard and then into the byre. We would let them rest awhile before taking them up by boat to the village.

The strategy for moving them was discussed over a cool beer in the kitchen. We would have to move each of the eight sheep singly from the byre, down the beach, into the rubber dinghy and out to the big boat. Lengths of baler twine were found and we moved amongst the sheep, caught them and trussed up their legs. I positioned the wheelbarrow outside the byre and Lachie and I heaved the first sheep into it. They were extremely heavy and the antiquated barrow wobbled precariously as we wheeled each sheep separately down to the beach. Four large woolly masses completely filled the dinghy and Lachie stood and rowed out while I perched among the prostrate bodies. Lifting them into the boat was harder and we each took a head or a bum and hauled them onto the deck. Luckily the tide was not racing.

Once they were all safely onboard, we set off for the village. Their shackles were cut and they huddled at the stern of the boat and crapped copiously over the beautiful, clean, pale, dove-grey deck.

The sun was setting and the wind had picked up significantly as we eventually pulled into the bay at the village. A

large swell was pounding the pier and it was going to be difficult to come alongside. Oh, for my old tyre fenders to save us
crashing against the concrete stanchions.

We were tied up and waiting for the right moment to heave
a sheep up onto the pier. The boat pitched up and down
considerably every time a wave passed beneath. The "up"
time would be the right moment to propel a captive ashore.
The boat plunged and we both grabbed as much body of a
sheep as we could through the huge fleece. The boat rode up
and together we flung the poor creature up and out onto the
pier. She stood and looked with wild eyes in the only way
that a frightened sheep can.

This procedure seemed to work and at the next wave crest
we heaved another sheep out. The deck by now was slimy
wet, very deep green and extremely slippery. We slithered
around in this container of shit trying to catch the final two
sheep, who both threatened to dive overboard to evade
capture.

All the time that we had been propelling sheep onto the
pier, there had been some very interested faces watching us
furtively from the pub windows, but of course nobody came
to help.

I waved goodbye to Lachie as the light started to fade and
headed out across the bay towards home. Once out in open
water, I let the boat steer herself and started to try and clean
up the mess. Many bucketfuls of sea water were sploshed
onto the deck and I swept the pungent goo out through the
scuppers. For some time after that day, the pale grey deck still
sported a shade of pastel green.

Lachie took the sheep home to his farm and restricted them
within a fenced field for a couple of months. This was to stop
them escaping and making their way back over the mountain

ranges to behind Caolas, where they had become accustomed to staying on one area of the hill; or in shepherds' language, they had "hefted" themselves.

Imagine my surprise when six months later I was on the top of the mountain and spied a small group of sheep just below the summit.

"Aye, that's them back again," Lachie said with quiet resignation, when I next saw him. "Must be nearly fifteen miles from my farm. Well the beggars can stay there this time."

Chapter Thirty-One

Stag Stalking

I pulled on my thick tweed breeches and fastened the button at the waist. They were a pale, greeny khaki colour with a faint red thread woven in one way at intervals in the material and a dull yellow thread woven the other way. The material would make ideal camouflage against the colours of the hill, for we were going deerstalking that day with our neighbours at the head of the loch.

The hills around Caolas carry a large quantity of red deer, which live completely wild and are free to roam wherever they want. Since the extinction by man of the last wild wolf in the eighteenth century, the deer have had no natural predators and in some areas populations have become very high to the detriment of their health. In harsh winters many of them starve to death. On all the large land estates around Caolas, good animal husbandry with sympathetic culling of weak and old beasts is undertaken, but still the population is high compared with a couple of centuries ago.

There is also the opportunity for guests to pay to go up into the hills with an experienced stalker and bag a "Trophy", a deer with a good set of antlers. This generates much needed income to help the running of the estates and pay the wages of local people who work there. Without deer stalking and management, our cottage wouldn't have been built and we wouldn't have had a job.

We would not be taking a trophy that day, but were after a beast seen recently with a poor set of antlers. It is known that the deer with superior antlers will pass these genes on to their offspring. There were a high number of excellent stags with "good heads" in the surrounding mountains.

Pete and I, together with Jeannie and her husband Iain, bumped up the long valley behind their house in their eight wheel drive Argo. There were two powerful rifles in their canvas bags and a box of ammunition. We had a lengthy climb ahead of us and it was a muggy day with the hint of warm sunshine. Already my thick tweeds felt very itchy.

Where the young river turned and flowed over a shingle bed, far beyond the "Women's pool", we left the vehicle and started to climb the hill. Iain was supremely fit and forged on ahead, soon leaving the rest of us struggling and panting behind. He was up in the hills most days stalking and knew the area well.

We caught up with him at the lip of a corrie as he was steadying his telescope against his stick and scanning the mountainside above us. He knew roughly where the stag would be, as he had spied it the day before from across the valley. It was running with only a couple of hinds. We had to avoid alarming any of the deer in the vicinity and a detour around the corrie was suggested. The ground was very broken and rough, with huge boulders blocking our way and long, tangling heather snatching at our legs as we tried to climb. The air was musky with the strong scent of the stags as we climbed on silently behind Iain. Flies and biting clegs, or horse flies, assaulted our sweaty faces and my breeches were stuck to my legs. We passed an odorous wallow where stags had recently thrashed about to coat themselves with the vile smelling mix of peat, mud and urine. This, in their eyes, made them appear even bigger and fiercer to an adversary.

Iain put up his hand and gestured for us to drop to the

ground. He crawled forwards for a few yards and parted the heather to spy ahead. Still crawling, now on elbows, we made our way slowly in single file along the hillside. All I could see ahead of me in the deep heather were Pete's wet boot soles and his tweed clad bottom wriggling as he writhed along on his belly. The wet undergrowth seeped moisture through my clothes and the wiry heather scratched at my face. People pay huge sums of money to do this, I pondered, as I annihilated another cleg.

A while later we stopped and Iain slowly and quietly un-shouldered his rifle and removed it from its case. He beckoned Pete alongside him with his own rifle. We had found our beast. Jeannie and I stayed silently low, my face uncomfortably close to a recent pungent deposit of deer turd. Pete took aim, his finger steady on the trigger and gently squeezed. The report of the powerful gun was astonishingly loud at such close quarters. The piercing blast echoed around the surrounding mountains and then faded. A stag reared up and fell backwards, his hinds scattering in blind panic.

"Good clean kill; well done," congratulated Iain.

We all stood up, brushed the loose undergrowth from our fronts and moved over to the dead animal. I was glad I hadn't been asked to pull the trigger. The deer was completely still, its eyes already glazing over. It was nearly a "switch"; that is, a stag that only has two straight antlers with no side points. This beast had only two points on each side. A good head would have six each side. Nobody would be mounting this head on a wall.

Iain took his sharp knife, held up one of the stag's hind legs and sliced along its belly. The warm guts burst out onto the ground; the huge stomach and the viscous slippery grey intestines. The shot had pierced the heart and lungs and these lay red and frothy still inside the beast. The "gralloch" would be left on the hillside, for it would feed the buzzards and foxes. Iain cleaned his knife on the wet grass and sheathed it again.

It was time to start the long drag down the mountain and back to the Argo. Ropes were tied to the hind legs and the head, fore and aft, so that two could pull at the front and, as I suspected, Jeannie and I would be the brakes at the back. We set off down. The men were pulling fast and we women found it difficult to keep pace. It was ankle breaking terrain, steep and rough, with the bloodied ropes threatening to slip through our hands. We smelt like stags now.

About halfway down, we stopped for a well-earned breather. A small cliff gave us shade from the warm afternoon sun and with blood and dirt-ingrained fingers, we ate our "pieces".

Iain's sharp eyes had detected some movement below us and he pointed downhill. A beautiful, russet-red dog fox, the size of a collie dog, was meandering amongst the rocks. We watched entranced as he pawed at small stones, turning them to see what was underneath, yawned and stretched, urinated and then continued padding his way out of sight.

Off again, we thundered down the incredibly steep hillside. The small Argo could be seen far below us and the pace was unremitting. My knees were like jelly, I was battered and bruised from falling against boulders and malodorous from collapsing on top of the carcass. We made it to the river as the sun was setting. I picked off a deer ked, a small disgusting insect that was climbing behind my ear, and washed my hands in the cool water.

We girls still had a long way to walk, because the stag would fully occupy the back of the Argo. The men and their cargo bounced off ahead. They would be back at the house long before us, but they would have to prepare the beast in the stag larder. There they would cut off the head and lower legs, take out the heart, lungs and liver and hang the stag ready for its journey the following Friday down the loch to the game dealer, who bought all the stags from the area.

Jeannie and I sauntered down the glen in the gathering dusky gloom. We were in no hurry now. We reflected on how, back before the Highland Clearances in the early 1800s, there had been a population of over a hundred people living in this glen. It must have looked vastly different then with their herds of small black cattle grazing where tall bracken now grew. The best ground was where the bracken always grew. These people, who had lived here for many years, were all savagely evicted by the landowner to make way for sheep. Many left on ships to start a new life across the Atlantic. It had been a sad and disgraceful time and the many ruined houses, the majority of them no more than a rickle of stones covered in undergrowth, stood testimony to past occupancy. Down at the shore, there was a small graveyard of uninscribed stones, indicative of the generations who had lived their simple, arduous lives there and maybe only really eked out a meagre existence. It was an evocative place and we walked on in contemplative silence.

Chapter Thirty-Two

Rutting Roars

"If that blooming stag doesn't shut up, I'm going to throw something at it," I said to the peaceful recumbent form lying next to me. How could he sleep with such an infernal, bloody noise just outside? The duvet continued to rise and fall gently and I sighed in exhausted frustration.

Now the sound of stags roaring their passion at the rut is a wonderful, exhilarating and spine-tingly experience and I knew we were honoured to have such an extravagant performance just below the bedroom window. However, this was the second night that this full throated baritone had given vent to his desires almost non-stop. Surely he must sleep sometime, even if he was feeling extremely randy.

I pulled the bed clothes up under my chin and tried to ignore the grunts and roars. The moon was shining in through the roof light and I watched as it traced a miniscule, slowly moving beam of light onto the back wall. Maybe an hour passed, but still sleep evaded me. A more distant stag started to call and what had been a relatively peaceful ten minutes erupted into a cacophony of ear-splitting roars.

The stag outside our house was so close that through the open window I could even hear his ragged intake of breath between bellows. I flung back the duvet and stomped to the window, stopping to pick up a sandal on the way. Silhouetted in the moonlight outside I could see several hinds grazing nonchalantly in the meadow between the cottage and the shore, but super stud was lying only yards from the front of the house. I waited quietly by the open window for some minutes. I could hear his coarse breathing. He was exhausted, the smell of his hot musky body wafted up on the still air to me. Maybe he would sleep now and give me some peace. I started to turn quietly from the window, just as he opened his mouth and gave a huge prolonged roar.

"Shut up and bugger off!" I flung the sandal as hard as I could. The hinds fled from the front of the house and, lumbering to his feet, my reason for insomnia trotted away, head held high.

In the morning after only a couple of hours of unbroken sleep, I found a dew damp sandal lying in the crushed grass. He took the hint after that night and moved his harem away, although maybe not too far

A week or so later, I was on my own at Caolas. There were no workers and Pete was away for a couple of days, so the dog and I had the place completely to ourselves. I had cooked myself a favourite supper that no one else seemed to like and sat down to listen to music by the roaring wood burner. With a generator it doesn't matter if you are running one light or twenty, it uses the same amount of fuel, so the house was lit up throughout. No more need to continue buying batteries to keep the radio going.

I stretched expansively and yawned. Barney raised his head momentarily; maybe he thought that it was an edible treat time. The cassette finished and the music faded to silence. It was time to take the dog out for his late night pee before bed.

It was then that I realised it wasn't going to be a quick foray out of the back door. A relay on the generator had stopped working the day before, which meant that the generator could not be switched on or off automatically from the house. I remembered with distaste the night before, when I was relaxed and ready for bed, having to squelch my way across the dark boggy field in pouring rain to switch it off.

"Come on old lad, let's go and shut the lights off."

I put my wellies on, grabbed a coat and a torch and we set off across to the generator shed. It wasn't raining and the massed light effect from the house pretty much lit up my way. Barney thought he was off for a walk and trotted ahead, pausing to cock his leg at clumps of reeds. The little generator "put-puttered" away in the shed, the noise invading the dark night. I opened the door and quickly flicked the switch off; the engine died, along with the Christmas tree effect at the cottage. Everything suddenly became so quiet and so black. With no other occupied dwellings, the complete darkness enveloped me. I put on the torch, called the dog and started to retrace my steps.

Now, have you ever been in a dark and lonely situation late at night when your imagination starts to play tricks on you? Your mind suddenly focuses on the faintest possibility that we could be visited by aliens; unsolved UFO sightings have been recorded. I walked a little faster. My mind replayed a scary film watched many years before where, through a black and oozing fog, slimy tentacles of some unseen monster slithered, grabbing unsuspecting humans by their ankles and dragging them off for ever.

"Oh don't be so stupid," I told myself firmly. "There is nothing out there to harm you."

My torch faltered and dimmed. The battery was low again. I stumbled onwards in the darkness with the dog at my heels. Suddenly, just off to my left, a huge roar broke the complete silence. I knew immediately it was a stag, but my super charged mind had already launched me into flight. Fleeing the last few yards to the dark cottage, Barney leaped joyfully up at me, he thought it was a game. I wrenched open the door, scurried inside and slammed it shut, then locked it. That door was never locked. Leaning heavily against the inside wall in the dark, my pulse was racing, but I was safe from the monster.

I was just regaining my breath when there was a scraping noise coming down the inside of the porch wall. All the fishing rods stacked in the corner had been dislodged by my slamming of the door and they cascaded randomly round my head and shoulders. Spinner hooks snagged firmly in my hair and coat, the rods flailing the dog as they reached the floor. He howled and fled. At the same time, the VHF radio in the corner of the kitchen crackled and I heard the voice of my friend Jeannie calling me. It was, of course, the time that she would call up to check if I was alright. We called each other at the same time every night. I couldn't move. I raised a hand to try and remove the most painful hook and impaled a finger on another hook.

"Jo, are you there?"

"I can't move," I muttered into the dark.

"Jo, are you OK?"

Dragging about six rods and their assortment of hooks by my hair, I shuffled over to the radio. With my only free hand, I lifted the receiver and pressed the transmit button.

"Hi, I'm fine," I gasped. The blood from my injured finger was dripping somewhere unseen onto the dark floor.

"You don't sound it."

"Oh it's nothing. I've just evaded the aliens and the slimy monster outside and have been now been savaged by the fishing rods."

There was a pause while she summed up the information.

"OK Jo," she replied in carefully measured tones, "but I really wouldn't have any more wine tonight."

We had a laugh about the quandary that I was in and she left me to disentangle myself in the pitch black.

It certainly was the stag's revenge that night after pelting my shoe at him.

Chapter Thirty-Three

Burns' Night

Only three more lengths of timber lining left to fix and I had finished the bedroom wall. The sounds of hammering emanating from up the corridor suggested that Pete was busy in another room. We had been working really hard on the interior of the big, old house and most of the rooms were formed with stud walls ready for the plaster and wood finish. I really enjoyed the carpentry and had, after showing an aptitude for it, been left to clad around the deep set windows with their awkward angles. The house was scheduled to be finished by the summer and would be used by our employer and his family for holidays. It had been decided, even after I was fit again, to keep on one of the workers, Ewan, who had been working alongside us for over a year.

It was time for a break and as it was coming up to Burns' night, we decided to take a trip up to the village and stay over for a night. All over Scotland people celebrate the works of the poet with a night of partying on 25th January. *Haggis and Neaps are traditionally eaten and the whole meal is toasted with several drams of whisky. (*Haggis is minced offal mixed with oatmeal and suet and traditionally boiled in a sheep's stomach. It sounds disgusting but is quite delicious).

The short afternoon was drawing on as we settled into the farmhouse kitchen up at the village. The boat was on the mooring in the bay and we had hitched a lift in a battered old Landrover the mile or so from the pier to the house. I had just made a cup of coffee and put on the lights when I heard heavy vehicles approaching up the rutted lane. On looking through the front window, I saw a strange procession slowly making its way past the house. In the front was Charlie driving the ancient tractor, which belched blue smoke out of its exhaust. He was towing a trailer on which there was a car perched precariously. Following was Johnnie in the yellow and rust JCB. The graveyard for dead cars was now further on past the farm and over the river.

It was obvious that this old fawn Renault was on its final journey. I had watched it on my last trip to the village, strangely weaving its way backwards full of provisions all the way down the road from the pier to the big house. Apparently, reverse was the sole remaining functioning gear.

The cortege passed, but not without hitting the large pothole, which caused the car to shift alarmingly. I wandered out of the door with my drink to watch the vehicles cross the river ford. It could be interesting as heavy overnight rains had swollen the waters. The tractor entered the ford and the peat brown water surged over the front wheels. Charlie was in danger of getting wet feet, but he ploughed on doggedly. The trailer bucked and bounced behind him and suddenly the old car slithered off the trailer sideways into the swirling flood. It lay there on its side completely blocking the ford, with the water gushing through the open windows.

Charlie pulled up on the other side and climbed down off the tractor. Something was shouted to Johnnie, who clambered out of the JCB and stood and lit a cigarette. I didn't think it was a good time to wander down and say "hello" so I furtively peeked around the corner of the barn. What were they to do? The light was fading and Charlie was stuck on the wrong side of the river and it was Burns' night with the promise of a good party. Some shouting and swearing followed, but their voices were almost drowned by the guttural uneven running of the JCB engine. It had needed new injectors for years.

After much altercation, Johnnie climbed back on the JCB, lowered the front bucket and drove with haste into the river. The bucket contacted with the flooded wreck and there was an awful noise of rending metal as he shunted it brutally over to the other side. The car toppled back onto its wheels, spewing water out of every crack and he kept shoving it sideways around the corner and out of sight. Charlie followed and picked up the bumpers and various bits that had become detached. There was no way they were going to miss the evening's entertainment.

When we eventually arrived at the pub, there was a fair crowd there already, with well-known faces we hadn't seen in some time. We sat with our drinks and chatted to friends as the local children raced up and down the floor. Charlie and Johnnie were already there with drams in front of them. The pub was doing a roaring trade. Someone from the kitchen came through to say that the haggis hadn't arrived yet by boat from town and we all peered through the misted windows to see if red and green boat lights were approaching. A short while later, lights appeared in the bay and several people went down to the pier to collect the meat.

The children were still boisterous and the drinks continued to flow over an hour later, when the celebrated haggis made its regal entrance on a large silver platter under a matching cover. Lachie, resplendent in full Highland dress, stepped forward, snatched up the lid and with his skian (knife) grasped in his hand, he addressed the steaming haggis. In the immortal words of Rabbie Burns,

> "His knife see rustic Labour dight,
> An' cut you up wi' ready sleight,
> Trenching your gushing entrails bright."
> He plunged the knife into the taut, rounded haggis.
> "O what a glorious sight,
> Warm-reeking, rich."

The steaming innards tumbled out onto the platter as he continued the address to the haggis, finishing off with.

"Gie her a haggis!"

We all cheered and whooped. His rendering had been awesome. The platter disappeared back into the kitchen and before long steaming plates arrived in front of us.

For some of the company, the wait had been too long. Pete and Johnnie sat slumbering together like a pair of bookends, their drams lined up in front of them.

Chapter Thirty-Four

Otter Island

Sitting on the warm turf bank at the edge of the bay seemed like a good idea. The grass roots lightly tickled the backs of my bare legs and my feet rested on large, round, sun-heated stones of the beach. I was waiting for the tide to recede far enough to walk out to the otter island, only accessible at a low spring tide, where I hoped to spy the otter family. On the way back, I had decided that I would pick some cockles for supper and my arm rested on an upturned bucket that I had brought with me for that purpose. Barney sat beside me and stared dreamily out to the loch, his nose twitching at some distant scent.

Oystercatchers, gathered at the edge of the water, called their shrill alarm and a small, ringed plover ran earnestly about on the pebbles below me, his "tuit" call giving away his well-camouflaged position. A light dry wind from the south east caressed the back of my head and the sun shone full in our faces. Slowly, inexorably, the water disappeared and the sandy and pebbly beach lay in front of us. The oystercatchers were far away now busying themselves at the water's edge as they sought tiny morsels of food.

"Come on Barney, let's go."

He yawned, stretched and jumped down off the bank. He loved coming to the beach and would always find a large stone to try and pick up, or a piece of driftwood to carry. As we walked over the beach, tiny fountains would spurt up in front of us as razor clams snapped shut and disappeared rapidly into the sand. There were the worm casts of lug worms and if I scuffed my foot along the beach, I uncovered dozens of cockles.

We reached the rocky island from the beach and clambered up its sea-weedy shore, as the tide had gone out sufficiently. Yellow vetches, wild thyme and thrift clung to the steep slope and large boulders hindered our way. Bracken and briars tugged painfully at my legs and I had to stamp a clear way through for the dog. We reached my spying place and I instructed Barney to lie quiet. With my binoculars, I scanned around the bay. A male and a female merganser were fishing just off the point; these beautifully coloured ducks are quite often seen out in the lochs, he with his crested dark green head and she with a deep chestnut one.

But what was that a bit further out? I adjusted the glasses to try and get a better view. It was a large bird sitting low in the water, rather like a cormorant, and it kept diving for quite long periods. I balanced the binoculars on a large boulder to try and keep them steady and miraculously the bird surfaced nearer. It was definitely a diver. Red throated divers could often be heard flying past and giving their sort of "cwuck cwuck" sound. This was far too large to be a Red Throat; it could only be a Great Northern diver. They are rare winter visitors who then fly off to breed in the Arctic, but a few stay on until summer in the north of Scotland. I could now see its white spotted back and the bands of white like a pearl necklace around his neck, for this was a male. What a thrill to see one so close to where we lived. I had come to see otters, but this was much rarer.

Time was moving on and I knew the tide would have turned, so reluctantly I left the diver to his fishing and Barney and I made our way off the island and back to the beach again before we were cut off. The otters had remained out of sight, probably basking somewhere near their holt.

With half a bucket full of cockles, we made our way home. Over the meadow we walked, across the burn with slippery stones and up the slope past the old house. The soft wind fluttered the leaves on the young trees in the enclosure around the generator shed. They were certainly growing well and one day in the future it would become a small wood. I wondered if I would ever see that.

Later on, as the sun was setting behind the high hills far down the loch, I sat outside and watched as the colours turned from gold on the opposite hills to deep shadows, with the sun only kissing the highest tops of the mountains at the head of the loch. A few stags ambled down and started grazing just along the meadow. What a privilege to have lived in such a pristine, unspoilt place. I turned reluctantly and a little wistfully back into the house and shut the door.

Chapter Thirty-Five

Dreams Don't Last

I couldn't stay at Caolas any longer. I was completely distraught. The wonderful dream that we had both embraced nearly four years before had become a nightmare and this beautiful place had become a prison. I was becoming trapped in an almost nightly conflict with an increasingly belligerent and drunken husband. Far from any help, I was alone and totally vulnerable. Sober, he was a talented, kind and generous man, but this changed with a few drams of whisky.

It was like living with two different people; a Jekyll and Hyde character. There was the daytime character who retained traits of the Pete I had loved and then there was the evening character, an incoherent wreck of a man who frightened and repulsed me. This untenable situation had gradually worsened in the previous four months.

During each day I managed somehow to push the memories of the previous night's confrontation to the back of my mind and prayed it would be different that evening. Blissfully, he sometimes remained reasonably sober. The weekends that I used to treasure so much as we would be just on our own, now became a particularly dreaded time.

We would drop Ewan off from work in port on a Friday and he would go home. Pete's drinking would start first in town and then increasingly on the boat home. Many times I had to try and manoeuvre a semi-comatose man off the boat in the narrows and ashore. I dare not leave him alone on the boat.

I now began to prefer the weekdays when Ewan was there, having his support and another human being in the house.

With great sadness, I realised that Pete and I had reached the end of the road together. Our marriage was over, just two months before our silver wedding anniversary.

The job was primarily Pete's and the house was tied to the job. If I couldn't live with him, then I would have to leave. That was the brutal reality.

When it happened, it was unplanned and immediate. I had no time to say goodbye to all the special places that I loved at Caolas. I left suddenly, carrying only a small holdall of clothes, my last view of my beloved home for four years disappearing astern as the boat carrying me sailed down the loch and away. Inconsolable tears were streaming down my face.

I had to leave Scotland and dear, long-term friends in Cornwall invited me to stay for a while with them and lick my emotional wounds. I had to try and figure out what I was going to do to earn a living and where I was going. My whole world had turned upside down. I only knew in that period of two months that I desperately wanted to get back to the west of Scotland; somewhere, anywhere, any job.

I wrote to friends in Scotland, I answered adverts for jobs in Scotland and was on the cusp of renting a cottage in Cornwall for the winter, when a phone call from some people I knew, amazingly made a return to Scotland possible. After two months, Barney and I made our way back up North again in an old Ford van that I had bought. We set up a new home in a wee tied cottage. I had to rebuild my life and friends provided a small job. It was a beautiful spot and helped to salve the pain of leaving dear Caolas.

Just as things were looking up, my faithful loyal Barney had to be put down. He had suffered a massive stroke and I cradled him in my arms as the vet gently pushed the needle in. He had been my dearest companion for fourteen years.

Nine months later, I was beginning to be optimistic about life again. I decided to take a long weekend camping trip up to northern Scotland and visit the island of Handa to see the puffins. I had been under canvas at a campsite on the mainland for several days and had neglected to listen to any radio news.

The small passenger boat from the mainland to the island was full of chattering people and through the snippets of conversation I heard a reference to a fire. There was a comparison to Gavin Maxwell, the writer and Camusfearna, whose remote cottage had burnt down some years previously. I noted these threads of conversation but didn't take too much notice.

Back at my car on the mainland that evening, I suddenly had an overwhelming urge to switch on the early evening Scottish radio news. It was unfathomable; a sort of dread premonition told me something was extremely wrong. There were the usual headlines of world events and then a headline about two men who had been killed in a fire at a remote cottage in western Scotland. It was in the area where I had lived.

I knew that it was surely someone I knew. I suddenly had a great fear that some of my friends had been killed, but whom? The main stories were read out in great detail; then came the sports news.

"Please hurry," I whispered. It seemed to take forever.

When the story finally came, the newscaster mentioned that the alarm had been raised by radio on board the boat the "Calypso" next to the burning cottage. My heart came up into my mouth. I gasped at the sheer horror of it, for I knew then that Pete had probably been killed. I stared dumfounded at the radio. What could I do to find out? There were no mobile phones then. Shaking like a leaf, I drove to the nearest house and pounded on the door.

"Please, can I use your phone?" I implored, explaining about the news.

On ringing friends, it was confirmed that indeed Pete and another man who was his friend had been killed in a horrific house fire at Caolas. They filled me in on the whole tragic story.

The alarm had been raised early that morning by a man called Harry, an eccentric loner who had, since I left, started living in a wooden shed on the far side of the narrows at Caolas. He had seen the smoke and rowed frantically across. As he raced to the cottage the flames engulfed the building. There was no hope of saving the two men, as the only fire pump had to come up the loch on the Lifeboat and that took over three quarters of an hour to come from the fishing port. The firemen and lifeboat men had battled in vain because the fire was too fierce.

The cottage was so badly destroyed that the fire investigators could not determine exactly how the fire had started, but I remember many times when I still lived there how Pete dropped his lit pipe on his chair as he became unconscious. Was that what had happened?

It was a sad and distressing time. I tormented myself with thoughts that if I'd stayed with him, I might have prevented this happening. I will never know. In all probability I could have been killed too. I knew in my heart that the day I left was an act of sheer self preservation.

It was all finished. I doubted then whether I would ever go back to visit Caolas. That amazing part of my life was completely over. The wonderful place with so many happy recollections, as well as sad, would only be in my memories from now on.

Chapter Thirty-Six

Forever Special

Nineteen years have passed and in all that time Caolas has remained in my mind. I have never stood on the shore, nor walked in the meadows, except in my thoughts. For a start, when I left, my thoughts were angry, so angry that I'd had to leave my lovely home and a life I relished and start out again. After Pete died, the anger diminished and changed to a feeling of great sadness. As the years have gone by, I have reflected on the times that we spent there, the happy as well as the sad, the frightening and the joyous. There has always remained a special place in my heart for this remote wild place and as the years passed, I vowed one day that I would return somehow and reacquaint myself.

It happened in early May all those years later, at the invitation of our past employer, who still owns and loves the place. I was thrilled to be going back, but I also felt great trepidation. Would the visit be too painful emotionally? My friends were very concerned about whether I was doing the right thing, but I felt an overwhelming need to go back there. It was with mixed emotions that I drove to the fishing port. My tummy was full of butterflies. Were my friends right? Was I making a huge mistake? What would happen if I couldn't stand being there after I was dropped off all alone? There would be no escape.

I was picked up by boat from the fishing port on a stunning spring evening. We sailed up the loch and, as if to welcome me, a school of porpoises swam by, their black fins breaking the surface of the water as they arched their bodies. I relaxed somewhat. It was still as beautiful as I remembered and then, oh my, there was Caolas far in the distance; the old house with the tree. My heart was thundering.

The boat gently crunched onto the shore and my box of food and rucksack unloaded. I stepped down onto the beach. It almost felt like a return from exile. I was back. My emotions were chaotic. I was ludicrously happy to be back at this spot, but also deeply sad because of the tragedy that had occurred. I stooped and picked up a round smooth stone from the beach and rolled it in my hand. It felt good.

The burnt cottage had been rebuilt many years previously and I walked towards it. It was going to be very strange to go inside again. Would I feel Pete's presence still there? I had always been sceptical about the supernatural, but there was something slightly unsettling about the fact that I would be staying all alone in the place where he had died so violently. I ran my hand along the old walls, undamaged by the fire, and felt a calm reassurance.

I stepped inside. It was so different and this was a huge relief. There was no resemblance to our old home and yet as I looked through the deep set windows, the view across the narrows was the same as I remembered; the wee cottage on the other side, the familiar mountains and the swirling tide in the narrows. The view was the same up to the head of the loch to the high peaks. Suddenly, it was as if all the years had rolled away and I had never left. I remembered it so well; those much loved hills, the meadow and the old house squat and sturdy with its attendant sycamore tree. I felt there was closure to a sad event, but also renewal, for I knew I could come back to visit anytime. My trepidation about the visit vanished as I sat on the doorstep whilst darkness fell.

The next morning, after a deep and peaceful sleep, I pushed open the roof window in my bedroom and took in the vista to the head of the loch. How many times had I greeted the morning the same way when I had lived there?

I spent the next few days with happy footsteps revisiting all the places that I loved. Yes, many things had changed. The tiny saplings that Pete and I had planted around the generator shed had matured into an impenetrable wood, with some trees thirty foot high. The wooden shed nestled in a glade and herons had chosen the highest trees for their untidy nests. The fenced area where we had kept the pigs and then grown vegetables had been planted as a wood in Pete's memory. I pulled open the gate and walked into this quiet reflective place. A path ran through the middle, bordered by blossom trees, cherry and apple, profusely in flower. Suddenly, in the undergrowth, I saw a small dilapidated shed. It was the tatty remains of the wooden chicken hut where we had shut Cedric and his ladies at night, away from the fox and pine marten.

It brought back so many happy memories. It was a lovely memorial wood and I took a cup of coffee in there on several occasions to just sit and reflect.

On the stairs of the cottage, there were some old black and white photos of past occupants of Caolas. I was fascinated. There was a picture of haymaking on the front meadow and stooks of cut oats in front of the cottage. A man and woman stood outside the cottage, accompanied by a tall, good looking son. Who were these people? I would have to find out. Maybe they would all be dead now, although the hay making photo showed a grey Ferguson tractor and mower and this could have possibly been taken after the last war. There were pictures of cows sitting cudding with the old house in the background. These were people who had made a living there once. I wondered if they had loved the place as much as I did. Their obvious hard work and dedication suggested that they did.

A pair of house martins were busy making a nest under the eaves of the cottage and zoomed in over my head as I sat on the bench outside the kitchen window. A cuckoo sang his repetitive "me-doh" song from the trees nearby and another answered "soh-me".

On one of the days, I wandered down to wild cat bay and on to magic wood. It was still the same as I remembered it; old gnarled oaks, burgeoning bracken and moss. The leaves were fresh spring green and the warblers sang sweetly from the high branches. I sat for ages just absorbing it and smelling the damp, earthy aromas.

On the way back I called at Jacuzzi pool, shaded by its ancient holly tree. It was surrounded by a wild garden of primrose, violets and the first bluebells. I contented myself by sitting by the cascade and drinking the soft sweet water.

A fox darted away as I crested the last rise before the flat meadows. He had been sitting in the sun. I walked back along the loch side to the piping calls of oystercatchers and the harsh squawks of diving terns. Later that evening, a snipe displayed and called over the peat bog behind, as a group of deer wandered down off the hill to spend the night grazing on the meadows.

I also visited the old house. I had left before it was completely finished. It was a lovely home now, full of furniture and treasured belongings. I touched and ran my hands along the walls that I had built. It was a special feeling that somehow linked me forever to the place. I had designed the house and it was wonderful to walk through and see the parts that I had fitted. Part of me would be there for many years to come; my link with Caolas.

I walked across the peat bog and saw the place where I had dug the peats. Someone had recently been digging at the same spot and there were dry peats piled onto a wooden pallet board. I hoped that the digger would forgive me, but I pinched a couple for my fire that evening.

Whilst over the bog, I decided to walk up to the water tank, an obscure thing you may think to do, unless you have been in the situation where you rely on local mountain water for your house. It was the same old tank wedged against the bank. I was suddenly aware of a horrible smell of a dead animal nearby and prayed it was not above the water inlet. On turning 'round, I gave an involuntary gasp for where I had helped a sick stag in the same spot many years earlier, there was now a decomposing carcass of a deer. It was a bit strange and I shuddered, for the deer that I had helped had recovered and moved by the next day and now all these years later there was a dead animal there. It gave me a creepy feeling and I was glad to get back to the flat ground.

The final evening came too soon. Another beautiful May day was ending with a stunning sunset. I sat on the bank near the old house as the shadows deepened around me. The sun had disappeared behind the mountains to the west and only the intense orange glow remained in the sky. Far above me, I suddenly caught sight of a Golden Eagle lazily circling right overhead. They still lived there. I wondered if it was a descendent of the pair that I had known, or maybe it could still be one of the eagles that I had known, for the lifespan of a Golden Eagle can be 30 years or more. A tiny sliver of a new moon rode high in the sky and the eagle passed in front of it. I sighed happily and let my hands rest on the short grass.

I suddenly experienced an eerie feeling that I was not alone. Nothing really tangible; just a feeling that had sprung out of nowhere. I felt as though something or someone was sitting with me. There had always been talk in port that Caolas was haunted. My thoughts immediately careered into the possibility that Pete's spirit was there with me. I hadn't felt anything all the time I was in the cottage. Maybe somehow I had wanted to make my peace with him and spirits did exist. But no, this feeling suddenly manifested itself into thoughts about Barney. Was it my beloved dog there with me? I called his name as if I expected him to appear. There was nothing; just an overwhelming feeling that he was close. How unexpected was that? We sat together as darkness closed around and the first stars glimmered above.

"I will be back again before too long," I murmured, for I intended to go back in the spring and plant a blossom tree in the memorial wood. All was at peace.

Lightning Source UK Ltd.
Milton Keynes UK
13 September 2010

159809UK00001B/7/P